Hooked on Writing!

Carol H. Behrman

Ready-to-Use Writing Process Activities for Grades 4-8

**THE CENTER FOR APPLIED
RESEARCH IN EDUCATION**
West Nyack, New York 10995

10   9   8   7   6   5   4   3   2

Excerpts from *Anne Frank: The Diary of a Young Girl*, by
Anne Frank, ©1952 by Otto H. Frank; used
by permission of Doubleday, a division of Bantam,
Doubleday, Dell Publishing Group, Inc.

Library of Congress Cataloging-in-Publication Data

Behrman, Carol H.
  Hooked on writing! : Ready-to-use writing process activities for
grades 4-8 / by Carol H. Behrman.
     p.   cm.
  ISBN 0-87628-409-8
  1. English language—Composition and exercises—Study and teaching
(Elementary) 2. Education, Elementary—Activity programs.
I. Center for Applied Research in Education.   II. Title.
LB1576.B426 1990   90-35901
372.6′34—dc20   CIP

ISBN   0-87628-409-8

THE CENTER FOR APPLIED
RESEARCH IN EDUCATION
BUSINESS & PROFESSIONAL DIVISION
A division of Simon & Schuster
West Nyack, New York 10995

Printed in the United States of America

To Edward,
with love

About the Author

Carol H. Behrman was born in Brooklyn, graduated from City College of New York, and attended Columbia University's Teachers' College where she majored in education. She married Edward Behrman, an accountant, and moved to Fair Lawn, New Jersey, where they raised three children and where they still reside. For many years, Behrman taught grades five through eight at the Glen Ridge Middle School where she created a program, utilizing the writing process, that combined language arts with typing and word processing instruction. She has written sixteen books, fiction and nonfiction, for children and young adults, and has conducted numerous workshops on the writing process for students, teachers, and aspiring writers. She is an adjunct lecturer at New York University's Writing Center.

About This Resource

Hooked on Writing! has been compiled *by* a classroom teacher *for* classroom teachers. All the Worksheets and projects have proven successful in actual experience with boys and girls in grades four through eight. With minor modifications, they can also be utilized for students somewhat younger or older.

The writing process is not a theory-laden fad cooked up in a university department of education and sent down from the ivory towers of academia to be dutifully applied by teachers in the front lines (where practice and theory often clash). The only new thing about process writing is the label. The procedures themselves have always been used in varying degrees and combinations by successful writing teachers. While the process of effective writing is fascinating and worthy of study, it is not necessary for the classroom teacher to be versed in every esoteric detail and nuance. It is enough to be aware of the steps involved and the best ways of using this knowledge for the specific group and project at hand.

Most students who are "naturally" good writers follow process writing steps even when they themselves are not aware that they are doing so. Oftentimes, these students are avid readers and have managed to absorb many techniques of good writing from well-written books. Poor student writers have failed to do this. They usually don't know why they are not successful and fail to understand how they can go about improving their skill. Too often, after enough failure, they don't even care. Like a fledgling cook, who has been provided with flour, shortening, sugar, and baking powder and then told to bake a cake without a recipe, the student writer often finds that knowledge of vocabulary, spelling, grammar, and sentence structure is not enough to turn out successful prose. They need to know the recipe. Process writing provides the student not only with a "recipe" for writing, but also with two enormously effective tools.

The first tool is motivation. When students are told that by learning a few simple steps they will be able to write more easily and successfully, when the teacher can assure them that this knowledge will make effective writers out of poor writers and help good writers to communicate even better, students are usually sparked with a renewed interest in written communication. All children have a great deal within themselves to express, both in terms of ideas and emotions. When they develop confidence in their writing abilities, they are ready to flood the world with words that portray their inner selves. Process writing readily lends itself to use with other effective motivational devices such as journal writing, student writer conferences, and publication, all of which will be discussed in greater detail in this book.

The other important tool that process writing gives to the learner is *control*. It is the *student* himself or herself who becomes the critic and evaluator. Rather than turning out a draft which is then corrected and red-penciled by the teacher for reasons the student doesn't always understand, the student assumes responsibility for seeing to it that the finished work effectively communicates what he or she wishes to say. Unsuccessful writers don't have the ability to see why their work is ineffective. The process method provides them with this skill. To some extent, the onus of being a judge is transferred from the teacher to the student. When this method is successfully applied, the teacher's job actually becomes easier, and his or her role becomes more that of a guide in the learning process. The sense of control that students acquire over their writing is a powerful aid in developing self-confidence and making writing an enjoyable and exciting activity, rather than one to be feared and dreaded.

There is little or no theory in the pages that follow. For each project, the steps are clearly delineated, the materials easily adaptable to various grade and learning levels, and the suggestions for use always specific and based on extensive testing with the classroom as laboratory. Most activities include convenient, time-saving reproducible worksheets grouped together at the end of each chapter. Enjoy!

Carol H. Behrman

Using the Stages of the Writing Process

The steps of the process writing method have been variously outlined and described. In general, they follow the pattern offered here, but the built-in flexibility of this system makes it easy for the teacher to rearrange, alter, omit, or substitute any of the stages in ways that will be appropriate to individual students, classes, or curricula. For example, some fourth and fifth graders might find the process too long and respond better if a few steps, such as one of the drafts or the second peer group critiquing, are omitted.

PREWRITING ACTIVITIES

Examples: Students should be shown at least one example of the type of writing involved, such as a poem, essay, newspaper article, or story, followed by a class discussion of the elements that make this piece successful.

Brainstorming: Group or individual brainstorming (or both) may be used depending on the nature of the assignment and the goals set by teacher or curriculum. Students should be encouraged to include whatever phrase, name, or idea the topic may bring to mind. There are no wrong answers in brainstorming. Every contribution is worthy of consideration, and may later be selected or discarded by the individual writer. Group brainstorming is particularly effective when the students are first learning this prewriting technique. Later, individual brainstorming lists are useful. It is advisable for these lists to be checked by the instructor before the actual first draft writing begins.

FIRST DRAFT: Encourage the students to write quickly, to put down each detail of the story, essay, or poem as it comes into their minds. Tell them not to be concerned at this point with spelling, grammar, or legibility. The purpose of the first draft is to write, write, write—to transfer the material taking shape in their thoughts onto the paper regardless of form.

GROUP CRITIQUING WORKSHOP: Divide the class into small groups of three or four. Advise the students that at this point they will be looking to see if the material makes sense, if the author has successfully communicated his or her ideas. As they read each other's work, tell them to be on the alert for spots where there is a lack of clarity. For example, in fiction, are they sure which character is speaking or being referred to? Are there places where the time frame is confusing (when did this happen)? Has the author omitted some details that are important for understanding the action? In an essay, is the point that the author is trying to make clear? Do the facts and examples support the thesis? Are they arranged in a way that leads the reader confidently and easily toward the author's conclusion? Poetry critiquing will depend on the form and style that the students are trying to achieve. The exact points that are to be critiqued on any piece of work will be determined by the particular activity being attempted. Usually, the writer knows what he or she is trying to communicate. When faced with a peer's comment that there is some confusion, the author will know where he or she has to make revisions.

SECOND DRAFT: The students will rework their stories, essays, poems, or other material with special attention to the sections where their critique groups had problems. The writers now have some understanding of where they have failed to communicate effectively and should, therefore, be able to improve the comprehensibility and effectiveness of their manuscripts. Crossing out and writing in margins or on the back of the paper is acceptable.

SECOND CRITIQUING SESSION: The students meet once again in their small peer groups to ascertain if they have been successful in correcting the area where there was previously a lack of clarity.

DISCUSSION OF LANGUAGE ENHANCERS: Before students work on the last draft, you may want to review the effective uses of language enhancers such as strong, active verbs, sensory imagery, similes, and metaphors. (There are ready-to-use lessons in this book which do this.) Instruct the students to make further revisions on their papers, replacing dull, passive verbs with active ones, using some sensory imagery and/or similes and metaphors, if desired.

FINAL DRAFT: For the first time, the students will rewrite the complete manuscript, incorporating all the revisions they have noted, and paying more attention to the use of correct spelling and sentence structure.

TEACHER INPUT: Now is the time for you to read and edit the students' work. For the most part, your corrections should be confined to spelling, grammar, sentence and paragraph structure. It is important to build the students' self-confidence in their writing by giving them a feeling of control over their creative work. The two group evaluations will have improved the manuscript over its initial presentation, and subsequent exercises in creative writing will build the students' skills in this area.

FINAL COPY: Students should be encouraged to write or type their final copies as neatly as possible. The importance of their creative writing efforts should be emphasized by eventual public display or, if possible, inclusion in some sort of publication.

PUBLISHING AND SHARING: The final writing products will offer more satisfaction to students if some procedure for sharing work is used, such as reading aloud, posting work, or inclusion in a school or other publication.

Note: For younger students, the second peer group meeting and draft may be omitted.

Table of Contents

Worksheets:

2-1 The Hero/Heroine ◆ 2-2 What If? ◆ 2-3A Creating a New World (Gr. 4–5) ◆ 2-3B Creating a New World (Gr. 6–8) ◆ 2-4A Place Description: Sensory Words ◆ 2-4B Place Description: Choosing a Place ◆ 2-4C Place Description: Brainstorming ◆ 2-5A Writing a Description of a Person ◆ 2-5B Personal Description: Brainstorming List ◆ 2-6A Fill-In Story: *Young Tom Turkey* ◆ 2-6B Fill-In Story: *A Scary Halloween* ◆ 2-6C Fill-In Story: *The Last Class* ◆ 2-7 A Day in the Life Of ◆ 2-9 Writing to a Picture

Worksheets:

3-1 Group Response Worksheet ◆ 3-1A Think Tank ◆ 3-1B More Think Tank ◆ 3-1C The Idea Tree ◆ 3-2A Selecting and Focusing ◆ 3-2B Writing a Personal Essay ◆ 3-3 Another Personal Essay ◆ 3-4 One, Two Three! ◆ 3-5A Dynamite Beginnings ◆ 3-5B Wrapping It Up ◆ 3-6 Ask the Expert ◆ 3-7A Making Changes ◆ 3-7B Making Bigger Changes ◆ 3-8A What Do You Think? ◆ 3-8B What Do You Think? ◆ 3-9A Expanding an Idea ◆ 3-9B Expanding an Idea

Worksheets:

4-1 Setting It Up ◆ 4-2 Active Verbs ◆ 4-4 Sensory Words ◆ 4-5A Similes ◆ 4-5B More Similes ◆ 4-6A Metaphors ◆ 4-6B More Metaphors ◆ 4-7 Descriptions ◆ 4-8A Dialogue: Who's Saying What? ◆ 4-8B Dialogue: Place and Action

1

UNLOCKING THE DOORS TO WRITTEN EXPRESSION

The ultimate case of writer's block is depicted in a wonderful scene from Stanley Kubrick's film, *The Shining*, where we finally get to see the manuscript pages of the novel that Jack Nicholson has been pounding out on his typewriter for hours on end, day after day. There are hundreds of sheets, each filled top to bottom with the same line, repeated again and again: "All work and no play makes Jack a dull boy."

Unlike the character portrayed by Nicholson, most victims of writer's block do not end up running amok, but the level of frustration it brings about is, indeed, exceedingly high. Ask any student who has ever confronted a blank sheet of paper that must be filled up, only to find that all messages from his or her brain have been completely and inexplicably shut off. Unfortunately, there are too many youngsters (oldsters, too) for whom writing is a form of torture second only to cold-turkey withdrawal from television. These students have somehow learned to regard written expression as their enemy. The idea that one can have fun with words is as inconceivable to them as an essay in Martian.

The exercises in this chapter have been selected for the express purpose of combating this widespread distaste for writing as dull, boring, and something to be stoically endured. They break through barriers and prejudices as painlessly as possible and introduce youngsters to the concept that words are infinitely fascinating and that playing with them can be a lot of fun.

The short and interesting writing activities that follow will go a long way toward overcoming resistance, passivity, past failures, and negativity toward writing. These should not be treated as formal writing assignments, but rather as games, puzzles, challenges. You will not want to use process writing steps for most of these projects. They are a preliminary step, a motivational device, to make words and writing exciting and fun, and to make students receptive to future writing assignments. They can be done in any order, and most include Worksheets with easy-to-comprehend directions.

Activity 1   STREAM OF CONSCIOUSNESS

This activity is sometimes called "automatic writing." It is an effective tool for breaking down barriers and long-standing blocks. Many students (and adults, too) have tremendous difficulty getting started with a writing project. Stream of consciousness writing puts no pressure on the writer to achieve specific goals, and makes it easier to get those all-important first words onto the paper.

PREWRITING ACTIVITIES

1. Begin by setting a quiet mood, conducive to concentration. Try to eliminate distracting sounds.

2. Distribute Worksheet 1-1 STREAM OF CONSCIOUSNESS. Read directions slowly in a low, soft voice. Emphasize the advantages of writing like a flowing stream, without pause. Suggest that if students' minds are completely blank, they can just write something like, "My mind is blank" or "I can't think of anything to write" or "I am writing, writing, writing." Even nonsense words are okay. The point of this exercise is to keep the pen or pencil moving.

3. Younger students will respond positively to a suggestion that they pretend to be robots. When the teacher turns on an imaginary switch, the robots must write without pause until the switch is turned off.

4. Do this exercise for about five minutes the first time. On subsequent days, increase the time gradually.

Activity 2   SASSY SENTENCES

PREWRITING ACTIVITIES

1. Elicit from students familiar sayings, in which all or most of the words begin with the same letter, such as, "Peter Piper picked a peck of pickled peppers..." or "She sells seashells by the seashore..."

2. Write the letter *A* on the chalkboard. Beneath it, write a sentence in which each word begins with an *A*. (e.g., "Annie Andrew's aunt ate an angry alligator").

3. Ask the class as a group to compose several more sentences in which each word begins with an *A*. Write them on the chalkboard.

4. Distribute Worksheet 1-2A SASSY SENTENCES. Instruct students to write a sentence next to each letter, beginning all or most of the words in that sentence with that letter.

5. After the Worksheets have been completed, have the students share their efforts by reading the sentences aloud.

6. Worksheet 1-2B MORE SASSY SENTENCES can be used at the teacher's discretion either in conjunction with the first Worksheet or as a fill-in exercise on some subsequent date.

Activity 3   SENTENCE BUILDING BLOCKS

PREWRITING ACTIVITIES

1. Tell the students you are going to provide them with a set of building blocks with which they can construct more interesting and vivid sentences.

2. Write the following list of "building blocks" on the chalkboard:
   WHEN
   SIZE OR COLOR
   PLACE
   NAME

3. Write a simple sentence on the chalkboard: "The baby cried."

4. Illustrate how this simple sentence can be expanded by adding one building block at a time. Write each new sentence on the chalkboard, as follows:

Last night, the baby cried. (adding *when*)
Last night, the *tiny* baby cried. (adding *size*)
Last night, the tiny baby cried *in her crib.* (adding *place*)
Last night, *Greta's* tiny baby cried in her crib. (adding a *name*)

5. Distribute Worksheet 1-3 SENTENCE BUILDING BLOCKS for students to complete.

6. Share results by reading aloud.

Activity 4   SIMILES

PREWRITING ACTIVITIES

1. Review similes. Give several examples.

2. Write on chalkboard: "as red as ———." Ask students to complete the phrase. Write several of their endings on the chalkboard.

3. Most, if not all, of the similes suggested by the class will probably be for four- or five-word phrases (i.e., "as red as a beet," "as red as a rose," "as red as blood," etc.). Encourage the students to come up with longer comparisons, possibly suggesting situations or action, such as "as red as my face when I dropped all my books on the first day of school" or "as red as a summer sunset on the lake." Write these contributions on the chalkboard.

4. Distribute Worksheet 1-4 SIMILES. Instruct the students to follow the directions on the Worksheet, including the sentences at the bottom.

5. When the Worksheet has been completed, share similes and sentences by reading aloud.

Activity 5   DYNAMIC DESCRIPTIONS!

PREWRITING ACTIVITIES

1. Write the word *family* on the chalkboard. Ask the students for words that can be used to describe the word *family* (adjectives), such as happy, battling, etc. Write the words on the chalkboard next to *family.*

2. Write the word *place* on the chalkboard. Use the same procedures as in item 1.

3. Do the same with the following words: *camp, spot, tent.*

4. Establish that all the base words are nouns and the descriptive words are adjectives.

5. Distribute Worksheet 1-5 DYNAMIC DESCRIPTIONS. Read the directions aloud. Be sure the students understand that they must first circle all the nouns on the Worksheet before rewriting the paragraphs. Urge the students to use unusual, humorous, even silly adjectives if they wish.

6. When the assignment has been completed, read aloud several samples for each paragraph to demonstrate the different effects that can be achieved through the use of descriptive words.

Activity 6   GETTING IDEAS: A MIND MASSAGE ────────────

PREWRITING ACTIVITIES

1. Ask the students what happens when a part of the body (i.e., arm, leg, back) is massaged. Replies may include, "It tingles," "The arm feels stronger," "You feel more alert, like waking up in the morning," etc.

2. Tell the students that their minds can also be made to feel stronger and more alert with "mental massages." Mental massages can be particularly helpful in stimulating the mind to think up interesting and original ideas. If nothing else, a mental massage can break through the block that often keeps a student from getting started on a writing project.

3. Inform the students that the tools for "mental massages" are words. Distribute Worksheet 1-6 GETTING IDEAS: A MIND MASSAGE.

4. Read directions aloud for the first part of the Worksheet. Emphasize that the students will be dealing only with the *circled* word. Spend no more than three to five minutes writing words and phrases in the box.

4. Read aloud the directions for the second part of the Worksheet. Encourage the students to come up with a title before they begin their story or essay. This will help them focus on their subject.

5. Process writing steps as outlined on pages ix-x will fit in nicely with this activity when the first draft has been completed. This is a handy project for introducing process writing, particularly peer group critiquing.

Activity 7   EXPANDED DEFINITIONS ────────────────

Competent writers feel comfortable with words. Words are friends, warm companions on the road to creative expression rather than cold, alien, elusive things to be searched for, agonized over, used briefly, and discarded. The purpose of this activity is to give young writers a glimpse of the beauty, power, and evocative nature of words.

PREWRITING ACTIVITIES

1. Write the word *green* on the chalkboard. Ask the students for a definition and write it on the board. It will probably be something like, "a color made by combining blue and yellow." Tell the students that this is merely a dictionary definition, that the word *green* can mean much more than that, such as "the smooth, gleaming surface of jade," or "the color of Scarlett O'Hara's eyes." These expanded meanings can arise from each person's individual experience. Ask the students to remember some things in their own lives that can be used to expand the definition of *green*. Encourage them to think of feelings as well as objects. Write their contributions on the chalkboard.

2. Distribute Worksheet 1-7 EXPANDED DEFINITIONS. Read the directions and example aloud. Encourage students to reach into their own lives and experiences to come up with expanded definitions of at least two of the words on the Worksheet.

3. When the Worksheet has been completed, share definitions by having students read them aloud. Discuss the way the meanings of words can vary for each person.

Activity 8   OPPOSITES ATTRACT

This activity offers students practice in recognizing words and their opposites. It also encourages them to consider more than one point of view.

PREWRITING ACTIVITIES

1. Write the following words on the chalkboard:

small	hard
up	loud
old	happy
weak	short
hot	cowardly
beautiful	smart

2. Elicit the opposite of each word. Write it next to that word on the board.

3. Tell the students that not only words, but entire sentences, and even paragraphs can have their opposites. Write the following sentences on the chalkboard:
   The old woman lived on the top floor.
   Elicit the opposite and write it on the chalkboard below the first sentence:
   The young man lived on the bottom floor. (Some purist scholars in your class may even wish to change *lived* to *died*.)

4. Distribute Worksheet 1-8 OPPOSITES ATTRACT. Read directions aloud.

5. When Worksheets have been completed, share them in class readings.

Activity 9   HOW TO

Teachers often complain about their students' inability to follow directions. This skill, however, seems like a snap when compared to student efforts to *give* directions. I sometimes imagine that those printed instructions one finds in cartons of toys, appliances, furniture, etc. that must be assembled by the purchaser have all been prepared by moonlighters from my seventh-grade classes.

This activity (How To) is designed to sharpen the precise language and thinking skills needed for writing directions.

PREWRITING ACTIVITIES

1. Ask students if they or their families have ever purchased something that had to be assembled, and had trouble following the instructions. The students will probably come up with a variety of stories about missing parts, leftover pieces, incoherent directions, and frustrated parents.

2. Elicit student experiences following recipe instructions when cooking. Discuss the importance of clear, step-by-step directions and the danger of omitting important details.

3. Distribute Worksheet 1-9 HOW TO. Read directions aloud.

4. Upon completion, test the effectiveness of some of the directions that can be tried out in the classroom. Have one student at a time read directions while others try to carry them out.

Activity 10 ACTIVE VERBS

One of the hallmarks of a good writer is his or her ability to use vivid, exciting language. Active verbs always create more interesting prose than do passive ones.

PREWRITING ACTIVITIES

1. Write the following sentence on the chalkboard:
   Judy went to the store.

2. Ask the students to substitute a word for *went* that would make Judy's action more specific and vivid. With encouragement, they will come up with an extensive list of active verbs, such as *rode, hurried, ambled, flew, stumbled, skipped, skated*, etc. Write the words on the chalkboard. Discuss the definition of an active verb.

3. Write the word *see* on the board. Develop a list of more active substitutes, such as *peer, glance, stare, gaze, notice, glare*, etc.

4. Do the same for *touch* (stroke, punch, pat, pinch, slap, etc.).

5. Distribute Worksheet 1-10 ACTIVE VERBS. Read the directions aloud.

6. After the Worksheet has been completed, compare students' uses of active verbs by reading sample revised paragraphs aloud.

Activity 11 FEELINGS

Most of us write more easily when the words arise from our own feelings and experiences. Even those who tend to keep their emotions to themselves can often let loose when encouraged to express their feelings about themselves and their lives, once they get beyond an initial reticence.

This simple but effective exercise helps students find the words to express their thoughts, because it is easy and fun to do. It helps them begin to find a flow in their writing through the immediacy of their own memories and feelings.

PREWRITING ACTIVITIES

1. Distribute Worksheet 1-11 FEELINGS. Read the directions aloud.

2. Encourage students to complete the sentences with whatever thought comes out of their own life experiences. If they prefer, however, to be humorous or outlandish, they should feel free to do so.

3. Students will enjoy sharing their sentences with the class (on a volunteer basis only) and comparing the individual differences in sentence endings.

STREAM OF CONSCIOUSNESS

DIRECTIONS: When the teacher tells you to begin, you will start writing in the space below. Write whatever comes into your head. It doesn't have to make sense. It doesn't have to be good writing. Just put down your thoughts as they occur. If you keep having the same thoughts, just write them over and over again. If you get distracted by something, write about the distraction. If, for some reason, you just cannot have any thoughts, don't give up, but write down the names of the things around you. If you KEEP WRITING, you will gradually find yourself relaxing into the words, and they will begin to flow from your pen more easily.

_____

_____

_____

_____

_____

_____

_____

_____

_____

_____

_____

_____

_____

_____

_____

_____

_____

_____

_____

© 1989, The Center for Applied Research in Education

SASSY SENTENCES

A <u>Annie Andrew's aunt ate an angry alligator. _____</u>

B _____

C _____

D _____

E _____

F _____

G _____

H _____

I _____

J _____

K _____

(1-2A)

MORE SASSY SENTENCES

Here are some more sassy sentences. How long a sentence can you write where every word begins with the same letter?

L _____

M _____

N _____

O _____

P _____

Q _____

R _____

S _____

T _____

U _____

V _____

W _____

(1-2B)

SENTENCE BUILDING BLOCKS

Example	*The baby cried.*
ADD WHEN	1. Last night, the baby cried.
ADD SIZE OR COLOR	2. Last night, the tiny baby cried.
NAME A PLACE	3. Last night, the tiny baby cried in her crib.
ADD A NAME	4. Last night, Greta's tiny baby cried in her crib.

A boy played.

ADD WHEN
1. A boy played in the afternoon

ADD SIZE OR COLOR
2. A little boy played in the afternoon

NAME A PLACE
3. A little boy played outside in the afternoon

ADD A NAME
4. A little boy named John played outside in the afternoon.

A man laughed.

ADD WHEN
1. A man laughed last night.

ADD SIZE OR COLOR
2. A big man laughed last night.

NAME A PLACE
3. A big man laughed last night at the store

ADD A NAME
4. A big man named Tom laughed last night at the store

The dish fell.

ADD WHEN
1. The dish fell yesterday.

ADD SIZE OR COLOR
2. The small dish fell yesterday.

NAME A PLACE
3. The small dish fell yesterday at home.

ADD A NAME
4. The small dish fell yesterday at home on Gracies head.

The car speeded.

ADD WHEN
1. The car speeded at 12:00 AM

ADD SIZE OR COLOR
2. The red car speeded at 12:00 AM

NAME A PLACE
3. The red car speeded at 12:00 AM on University street.

ADD A NAME
4. The red Toyota speeded at 12:00 AM on University St.

Name_____   Date_____

SIMILES

DIRECTIONS: Complete the following similes.

1. as red as _a rose_
2. as cold as _Ice_
3. as hot as _lava_
4. as black as _night_
5. as white as _snow_
6. as green as _grass_
7. as bright as _the sun_
8. as dark as _black_
9. as fast as _lightning_
10. as slow as _a turtle_
11. as tall as _a ladder_
12. as tiny as _a mouse_
13. as sleepy as _Sleeping Beuty_
14. as timid as _bashful_
15. as brave as _a lion_
16. as cheerful as _Asyah_
17. as noisy as _birds_

18. as gloomy as _rain_
19. as loud as _thunder_
20. as hard as _rock_
21. as soft as _feathers_
22. as low as _the earth's core_
23. as high as _the Empire state buildin_
24. as stupid as ~~____~~ _dummies_
25. as smart as _a computer_
26. as wet as _water_
27. as dry as _a desert_
28. as smooth as _silk_
29. as rough as _sand_
30. as cruel as _death_
31. as kind as _a flower_
32. as ugly as _dirt_
33. as beautiful as _the sunset_
34. as thrilling as _a rollercoaster_

Now, write three sentences below. Each sentence should contain at least one simile.

1. _As we traveled we became as hungry_
2. _When we saw the bear we became a_
3. _When slavery had stopped we became_

DYNAMIC DESCRIPTIONS

DIRECTIONS: Circle each noun in the following paragraphs. Think of an adjective to describe the noun. Then, on a separate paper, rewrite the paragraphs using your added adjectives.

1. The family found a place to camp. The campsite was in a clearing surrounded by woods. The parents began to set up their tent. The children gathered wood for a fire. Then, they began to explore their surroundings. They ran down a path that led through the woods to a lake. There were boats in the lake and on the beach. It was great to be on this vacation!

2. The teacher stood at the front of the room. She was holding chalk in her hand. She wrote a sentence on the board. The teacher asked a question about the sentence. She called on Betty to answer the question. Betty wasn't listening to the teacher. She was thinking about her grandmother in the hospital. Betty couldn't answer the question.

3. It was two days till Halloween. Philip was looking forward to this holiday. He always went out trick-or-treating with his friend, Jimmy. Philip looked in his closet and took out his costume. He tried the costume on, but it didn't fit. He told his mother. They went to the store and bought a costume. When the day arrived, Philip put on his costume and was all set to go out with his friend.

bear
fierce as a lion
free as a bird.

GETTING IDEAS: A MIND MASSAGE

1. Circle one of the words below. Then, in the box, write any words, phrases, names, places, ideas, etc. that this word brings to mind. Don't think about it too much. Just write down quickly whatever comes into your head, even if it seems ridiculous.

   ANGRY   AFRAID   ASHAMED

2. Now, examine what you have written in the box. Does it give you any ideas for a story (fiction) or essay (non-fiction)? It could be something as simple as the memory of an event in your life. In the space below, write the title and then a first draft of at least one paragraph. You will probably find it helpful to use some of the words in the box above, but it is not necessary. (Use the back of this Worksheet if you need more room for your draft.)

⎯⎯⎯⎯⎯⎯⎯⎯⎯⎯⎯⎯⎯⎯

⎯⎯⎯⎯⎯⎯⎯⎯⎯⎯⎯⎯⎯⎯⎯⎯⎯⎯⎯⎯⎯⎯⎯⎯⎯⎯⎯⎯⎯⎯⎯⎯

⎯⎯⎯⎯⎯⎯⎯⎯⎯⎯⎯⎯⎯⎯⎯⎯⎯⎯⎯⎯⎯⎯⎯⎯⎯⎯⎯⎯⎯⎯⎯⎯

⎯⎯⎯⎯⎯⎯⎯⎯⎯⎯⎯⎯⎯⎯⎯⎯⎯⎯⎯⎯⎯⎯⎯⎯⎯⎯⎯⎯⎯⎯⎯⎯

⎯⎯⎯⎯⎯⎯⎯⎯⎯⎯⎯⎯⎯⎯⎯⎯⎯⎯⎯⎯⎯⎯⎯⎯⎯⎯⎯⎯⎯⎯⎯⎯

⎯⎯⎯⎯⎯⎯⎯⎯⎯⎯⎯⎯⎯⎯⎯⎯⎯⎯⎯⎯⎯⎯⎯⎯⎯⎯⎯⎯⎯⎯⎯⎯

⎯⎯⎯⎯⎯⎯⎯⎯⎯⎯⎯⎯⎯⎯⎯⎯⎯⎯⎯⎯⎯⎯⎯⎯⎯⎯⎯⎯⎯⎯⎯⎯

⎯⎯⎯⎯⎯⎯⎯⎯⎯⎯⎯⎯⎯⎯⎯⎯⎯⎯⎯⎯⎯⎯⎯⎯⎯⎯⎯⎯⎯⎯⎯⎯

⎯⎯⎯⎯⎯⎯⎯⎯⎯⎯⎯⎯⎯⎯⎯⎯⎯⎯⎯⎯⎯⎯⎯⎯⎯⎯⎯⎯⎯⎯⎯⎯

EXPANDED DEFINITIONS

DIRECTIONS: The selection below is someone's personal, individual concept (not dictionary definition) of the word *Thanksgiving*.

> Thanksgiving: the excitement of getting dressed up in our best clothes; the trip to my grandparents' house, with everyone talking at once about the delicious food to come; all the aunts and uncles and cousins crowding the small house like a hive with too many bees; every adult telling me how much I've grown since last year, and how annoyed I feel by the third time; the mouth-watering aromas coming from the kitchen that make me feel I'm going to die if I don't eat something soon; my grandparents' dining room table laid out with a crisp white tablecloth, gleaming silver and sparkling glasses; feeling secure and loved and belonging when we all bend our heads for grace.

This is not a dictionary definition of *Thanksgiving*. It comes from the writer's own feelings and memories about the word. Choose at least two of the words below. For each one, draw on your own thoughts and experiences to write a personal definition of that word. Begin in the space below and use additional paper if you need it. Circle the words you have selected. (You may do more than two if you wish.)

happiness	Halloween	American
horrible	embarrassing	fun
summer	winter	difficult
scared	friendship	cruel

_____

_____

_____

_____

_____

_____

_____

_____

_____

_____

_____

OPPOSITES ATTRACT

PART ONE—SENTENCES: Below each sentence, write another sentence that says the opposite.

1. Children love to do homework.

_____

2. Last winter was cold and stormy.

_____

3. That house is big and ugly.

_____

4. I saw a man with a thin face and long, skinny arms.

_____

5. This long assignment is difficult, but exciting.

_____

6. A huge crowd gathered outside the old senate building.

_____

7. The runner's legs felt tired, but his will was strong.

_____

PART TWO—PARAGRAPH: The following news story is not correct. What actually occurred is the exact opposite of what is reported in the story. Can you rewrite this article as it really happened? (Use a separate sheet of paper.)

Yesterday morning, an unusual event occurred at the fountain in front of the municipal building. Several young men jumped into the pool with their shoes on and stayed there for a long time. The police arrived and arrested the young men, who claimed that they were only trying to get relief from the intense heat of the summer day.

HOW TO

DIRECTIONS: Have you ever thought about the specific steps involved in performing even simple tasks such as tying a shoe, putting on a jacket, or brushing your teeth? In giving directions for these and other activities, you must be careful not to leave out any part of the process.

Write out instructions for one of the activities below. Do not take anything for granted. Pretend that the reader has never done this and does not have the slightest idea how to go about it. You must provide perfect, step-by-step, easy-to-understand directions.

tying a shoelace	brushing your teeth
putting on a jacket	driving a car
grilling a hamburger	painting a picture
making a bed	using a computer
operating a washing machine	riding a bicycle

_____

_____

_____

_____

_____

_____

_____

_____

_____

_____

_____

_____

ACTIVE VERBS

Writing can be made more interesting with the use of active verbs. *Rush* or *stumble* is more exciting than *go*. *Glare* or *squint* is more vivid than *see*.

Circle the verbs in the following story. Then, rewrite the story below, substituting action verbs wherever possible for the passive ones.

Jeff saw the mess in the kitchen. He went into the hall and took his jacket from the hook.

Then he went outside. He got on his bike, and went down the street to his friend Andy's

house. Andy was in the front yard. Jeff got off his bike.

"Hi, Andy," he said.

"What's up, Jeff?" said Andy.

Jeff moved closer to Andy. "I'm in big trouble," he said.

Andy looked at him. "You are?"

"Yeah," said Jeff. "I was going through the kitchen and I accidentally pushed over my

mom's favorite china casserole. It went on the floor and is in a million little pieces."

"Yeah," said Andy. "You're in big trouble."

_____

_____

_____

_____

_____

_____

_____

_____

_____

_____

_____

_____

FEELINGS

DIRECTIONS: Complete each of the sentences below.

1. I feel sad when _____

2. I am happiest when _____

3. I was embarrassed when _____

4. The funniest thing I ever saw was _____

5. My family _____

6. I like to _____

7. I hate to _____

8. Friends are _____

9. One summer, I _____

10. I was really disappointed when _____

11. It is exciting to _____

12. Once, I saw _____

13. It is hard for me to _____

14. It is usually easy for me to _____

15. I never _____

16. I always _____

17. I wish _____

18. The worst thing that ever happened to me was _____

19. Next year, I will _____

20. When I grow up _____

2

CREATIVE
WRITING

All writing is, or should be, creative. The term *creative writing*, however, is often used to refer specifically to the production of fiction, and this is how it will be treated in this chapter.

Most children love to write fiction. The wilder, the more far-out, or the sillier it is, the more they seem to enjoy it. This is also an area where students have less hesitation sharing their work with others than they do with more personal forms such as journals or essays. For this reason, fiction writing is an excellent area for working with students in small peer workshop groups, where they can learn critiquing skills by noting the flaws in the work of other students and also seeing where they themselves have failed to communicate what was in their minds as they were writing.

The greatest difficulty students seem to have with fiction writing is getting started. When faced with a creative writing assignment, minds often go blank. The first project discussed here is one which has proven successful in unlimbering both the mind and the hand that holds the pen. It is nonthreatening, easy to get into, and can be used with any age group.

Activity 1   THE HERO/HEROINE

PREWRITING ACTIVITIES

1. Ask students to name some characters they have liked in stories, films, or on TV. Answers will range from Nancy Drew to Encyclopedia Brown to Rambo to Indiana Jones. Discuss the reasons they admire these heroes/heroines.

2. Ask the students to make a list of characteristics that appeal to them, such as bravery, humor, cleverness, etc. Read the lists aloud. Discuss similarities and differences. Point out that each student probably wishes that he or she could be more like these idols. Tell them that, as writers, they have the power to re-create themselves in stories. By making themselves the heroes/heroines of a story, they can move closer to their ideals (on paper, at least).

3. Build student confidence by emphasizing how easy the first creative writing assignment will be. They are not going to write a complete story, but merely create a character based partly on themselves and partly on their ideal heroes. The character will have the same first name as the writer. In other respects (age, appearance, personality, abilities, etc.) he or she can be like or unlike the writer.

4. Distribute Worksheet 2-1 THE HERO/HEROINE. By following the directions on the Worksheet, the students will be able to turn themselves into heroes, regardless of their writing ability.

Use process writing critiquing and revising steps with this assignment (see introduction). Save the final versions to be incorporated into future stories.

Activity 2   GETTING IDEAS

PREWRITING ACTIVITIES

1. DEVELOPING AWARENESS

A. Point out to the students that there are objects and events all about them which can be springboards to story ideas, but all too often, people are not really aware of their surroundings. Ask the students to describe some objects in or near the school that you know that they probably pass every day. For example, you might ask them to describe the shape of a display of bushes in front of the school, or the color of some part of the building's exterior. Few students, if any, will be able to do so. This will startle and awaken them to their lack of awareness.

B. Next, have the students look around the classroom to see if they can point out things they have never noticed before. The more they look, the more objects they will admit to noticing for the first time. Perhaps they will exclaim over a peeling ceiling, a loudspeaker on the wall, a radiator, pipes, pictures, etc. Students of all ages usually get into this activity with gusto, and you may have to call a halt before they have completely finished calling attention to never-before seen phenomena.

C. In this connection, I have found that students are usually fascinated by hearing about a story from Aldous Huxley's novel *Island*. This is a book about an ideal society, living on an island completely out of contact with, and safe from contamination by, the rest of civilization. This society has developed a culture based on gentleness, love, and individual fulfillment. On this island lives a most unusual bird that flies over the island constantly. It is a talking bird, but can say only one word—"Attention!" It flies about the island constantly, calling down to the people below, "Attention! Attention!" At this point, you can ask the students to think about the exercise they have just done and to try and guess what the bird means by, "Attention!" They don't always make the connection immediately, but with a bit of direction, usually at least one student will eventually come up with the correct answer—that the bird is telling the inhabitants to pay attention to the moment, to really notice what is around them.

2. *WHAT IF?* ACTIVITIES

A. The next step is to work with the students on developing story ideas from some of these everyday objects and events. Here, you can introduce two "magic words." These words are *what if?*. For example, point to a loudspeaker on the wall and say, "*What if* that speaker really works in reverse? Instead of messages coming into the classroom, the speaker is in fact taking in everything being said and done in the room, and sending it through a series of wires to a house down the block. *What if* there are spies in that house listening to what is going on in the classroom? They might be spies hired by your parents, who are now aware of all that you say or do in class. Which parents are these? Who are the spies? What will happen when you get home?" You can relate a few more *what if* scenarios, but it will not usually be necessary to do more than one or two. When you next point to some object in the room, some student will surely be ready to come up with his or her own *what if* script.

B. A class discussion can follow, with students making up story ideas from the objects around them until there are enough story ideas for writing to begin.

3. Tell the students that they can use one of the ideas mentioned during the discussion or can make up their own. Distribute Worksheet 2-2 WHAT IF?. Direct the students to follow these steps:

A. Answer briefly the questions at the top of the Worksheet. (This will help them focus their story.)

B. Refer to Worksheet 2-1 THE HERO/HEROINE. Direct the students to begin the new story with a description of the main character. Then place him or her in the setting where the *What If?* story is taking place.

4. When first drafts have been completed, follow process writing activities (group critiquing, revisions, etc.).

Activity 3   CREATING A NEW WORLD

PREWRITING ACTIVITIES

1. Two Worksheets are offered (2-3A and 2-3B CREATING A NEW WORLD). One is suitable for grades four and five, the other for grades six, seven, and eight. Distribute the appropriate Worksheet.

2. Read the directions aloud. Discuss the suggestions on the Worksheet and offer some examples of how these could be implemented in a story.

3. Ask the students to contribute ideas for possible names for an imaginary place. Write place names on chalkboard.

4. Emphasize to the students that these stories are most interesting with lots of details and descriptions.

5. Instruct the students when writing their first draft to concentrate on getting their ideas down on paper regardless of spelling, grammar, etc.

6. Students write the first draft.

7. When the first draft has been completed, follow the process writing procedures (group critiquing, subsequent drafts, etc.).

Activity 4   PLACE DESCRIPTIONS

Students often have difficulty incorporating descriptions into their writing. In their own minds, they know what the places and people in their stories look like. They don't realize, however, that the reader does not have this information and, therefore, they tend to omit it.

PREWRITING ACTIVITIES

1. Descriptive writing is often enhanced by the judicious use of colorful adjectives, sensory words, similes, and metaphors. Before commencing this project, therefore, it would be helpful to hold a brief review of these, if for no other reason than to give the students a palette of colorful, exciting words. If there is not time to review all of them, concentrate on a discussion of sensory words, as these are particularly useful in descriptions. Write the five senses (touch, taste, smell, sight, sound) on the chalkboard. Compile a short list under each category.

2. Read aloud the following example of a place description:

The rose garden was a sweet-smelling enclosure far out on the rear grounds. The circular garden was formed by the bushes—a round tangle of roses of every type and color. There were climbers and ramblers and tea roses—reds, pinks, yellows, and whites. In the center was a grassy clearing, completely hidden from the house by the tight knot of thorny bushes. There was a white wrought-iron bench on the grass, decorated with carvings of roses. Jennie felt more comfortable here than anywhere. There was a sort of warmth about the place.

3. Discuss with the students how a description is like painting a picture with words. Write on the chalkboard some of the words and phrases in the above description that make this scene vivid to the reader: *sweet-smelling, circular, round tangle, tight knot of thorny bushes, white wrought-iron,* etc. Encourage the students to use as many sensory words as possible in their own descriptions.

4. Distribute Worksheet 2-4A SENSORY WORDS. Read the directions aloud. Have students complete the Worksheet, and then share the results.

5. Choosing a place: Distribute Worksheet 2-4B. Read the suggested subjects aloud and discuss them. Add other possible subjects and/or elicit ideas from the students. Have students write the name of their subject on the Worksheet.

6. Brainstorming: Discuss with the students how the use of brainstorming lists makes the actual writing much easier. Practice by having the class, brainstorming together, come up with lists for several topics suggested by the teacher, (e.g., "Cafeteria Food," "Halloween," etc.). Write lists on the chalkboard.

7. Distribute Worksheet 2-4C BRAINSTORMING. Read the directions aloud. Check each student's brainstorming list before going on to writing the description.

8. When the first drafts have been completed, have the students meet in peer-critiquing groups and then work on revisions.

9. (Optional) Students in grades 4 and 5 may wish to illustrate their final copies.

Activity 5   PERSONAL DESCRIPTION

PREWRITING ACTIVITIES

1. Review use of adjectives and sensory words in descriptions, as discussed for place description (CREATIVE WRITING ACTIVITY 4).

2. Distribute Worksheet 2-5A WRITING A DESCRIPTION OF A PERSON. Read aloud and discuss. Emphasize the need to describe a subject in such a way that he or she can be identified from the description alone. The students will decide on their subject at this time, but will not begin their first draft until they complete the brainstorming list, as described next.

3. Distribute Worksheet 2-5B BRAINSTORMING. Read the directions aloud. Have students complete the Worksheet and show it to you before beginning the first draft of description on a separate sheet of paper.

4. When first drafts of descriptions are completed, students will read them aloud without giving away the name of the subject. The rest of the class will try to guess the subject's identity. Group critiquing and revisions can be done after this "guess who?" game has been completed.

Activity 6   FILL-IN STORIES

Fill-in stories are an effective motivational tool for creative writing. They are useful for students of all levels of writing ability. For the reluctant writer, they provide an opportunity to feel successful in a writing assignment. For the capable writer, they stimulate creativity. They offer the satisfaction of creating an original story in an easy, painless manner. All students find them fun to do. There are many options as to how students will steer the basic narrative—they can bring in humor, excitement, adventure, terror, or joy.

The fill-in Worksheets 2-6A, B, and C are most appropriate for students in grades four, five, and six. Seventh- and eighth-graders, however, enjoy working on them, too. For these older students, fill-in stories can be especially useful during the sometimes "itchy" hours just preceding a holiday or vacation. For this reason, the fill-in stories presented here are mostly of a seasonal variety.

Since the primary purpose of this device is to motivate and stimulate a positive attitude toward writing, it is best to omit all steps of the process method here. No drafts and no revisions, please—just a few enjoyable moments having fun with writing.

Most writers, especially younger ones, will enjoy sharing and comparing their completed stories with those of their classmates.

Activity 7   A DAY IN THE LIFE OF

This is another writing project that works well at all grade levels, four through eight. The work of the older students will, of course, be more sophisticated, but boys and girls of all ages will find it fun to do. Many get so involved in the identity of the object, animal, or person about whom they are writing that they turn out truly imaginative and perceptive work.

For this exercise, as well as most of the others in this book, the students' writing skills will benefit if students are taken through the critiquing and revising steps of the process method. The extent to which this is done with each project will depend on the ability and needs of the group, the time available, and your goals for that particular writing project.

PREWRITING ACTIVITIES

1. Give something like the following directions:

   You know what your day is like from the time you rise in the morning until you go to sleep at night. Have you ever thought how the twenty-four hours of a day seem to your dog? What does the world and all the things that occur during a day seem like from the perspective of a dog? Or a cat? Or a monkey in the monkey house of the zoo? What is it like for your baby brother in his crib, who can't even talk yet? It's even fun to think about what a day is like for common objects, such as the chalkboard at the front of your classroom. What is it like to be written on and erased? Does the chalkboard learn from the words and numbers written on it? What does it feel like to be scratched with chalk? What about the bulletin board? How does it feel to be stuck with thumbtacks? Are some people more gentle than others when stabbing you? What does the bulletin board think of all the displays that are changed from time to time? You might want to write from the point of view of a typewriter, or the computer in the school office. How about the piano in the music room, or a classroom door, or the refrigerator in your kitchen at home?

2. Distribute Worksheet 2-7 A DAY IN THE LIFE OF. Instruct the students to select one of the choices already discussed, or pick another subject, and complete the title at the top of the Worksheet.

3. Discuss the brainstorming section of the Worksheet. Read the directions aloud. Students should show their brainstorming lists to the teacher before commencing the first draft.

4. Urge the students to use a lot of detail, action words, and sensory words, and tell about a whole day in the life of this subject from early in the morning until late at night.

5. After the first draft has been completed, follow the process method for group critiquing, revisions, etc.

Activity 8   WRITING TO MUSIC

PREWRITING ACTIVITIES

1. Instruct the students to relax, to close their eyes, and even, if they wish, to put their heads down on their desks. (The students will love this, thinking it a good way to goof off.) The purpose, however, is to shut out visual distractions and enable the students to concentrate on the music. Instruct the students not to force thinking but to allow free entry into their minds of whatever scenes, feelings, and ideas the music might bring. Keep your voice soft and low.

2. Choice of music: Take your own preferences into account. Children will tune in very quickly to boredom or lack of enthusiasm on the teacher's part, and are quick to pick up a teacher's excitement about and identification with the music. For pure effectiveness in stimulating creative writing, I have found portions of the following music to work well: Rimsky-Korsakov's "Scheherazade," Saint-Saens's "Danse Macabre," Rossini's "Overture to William Tell," the closing section of Tchaikovsky's "1812 Overture," Moussorgsky's "Pictures from an Exhibition," Prokofiev's "Peter and the Wolf," Tchaikovsky's "Nutcracker Suite," Richard Strauss's "Also Sprach Zarathustra" (the theme from the film *2001*), and a variety of selections from modern electronic music.

3. Turn on the record or cassette. Play the music fairly loud so as to drown out other sounds. Don't let the music go on too long. (You don't want them to fall asleep, do you?) Five to ten minutes is sufficient. Then, tell the students to begin writing immediately while their reactions are still fresh in their minds.

4. Tell them to describe their thoughts and feelings with as much sensory detail as possible. If they are describing a scene, don't forget colors and shapes and other details. Perhaps the scene or feelings can lead to a story idea. If so, encourage them to begin the narrative.

5. You might wish to offer several musical experiences during a class period, have the students write briefly about each one, and then choose the one that excites them the most to expand on.

6. After writing, divide into small critiquing groups to share and discuss students' work before revising. They will be intrigued (as will be the teacher) with the variety of different responses to the same musical stimulus.

Activity 9   WRITING TO PICTURES

Pictures can provide an excellent source of story ideas. One picture can be used for the whole class (with the help of an overhead projector), or several can be displayed and the student writers may choose among them. If magazine tearouts are used, each student may be given his or her own picture from which to work. Some periodicals that contain unusual pictures that may stimulate imaginative writing are *National Geographic, Psychology Today* (this magazine often contains very weird pictures which the children love), *Smithsonian Magazine, Life, Sports Illustrated, American Photographer,* and *People*. Good illustrations, including advertisements, can be found in almost any magazine. If you would like to add an educational dimension, reproductions of the works of well-known artists may be used. Museum art postcards can be effectively used for this purpose. Some examples of modern art can be particularly stimulating in encouraging story ideas.

PREWRITING ACTIVITIES

1. Display picture(s) to be used for the entire class, or distribute individual pictures. It is best to use pictures showing at least several people and/or animals and some interesting or even outlandish detail in the background to provide the writers with characters and props for the story.

2. Distribute Worksheet 2-9 WRITING TO A PICTURE. This Worksheet offers detailed brainstorming exercises for this project, and is particularly useful in helping students to delineate specific characters and a plot. The same Worksheet can be used for all grades.

3. When the first draft has been completed, follow process writing steps for critiquing, revising, etc.

Activity 10   SOME SHORT CREATIVE WRITING PROJECTS ————

Following are some additional projects you may wish to use. They are all short, and most will take only one classroom period to complete. No Worksheets are needed.

BECOMING SOMEONE ELSE

TEACHER'S DIRECTIONS: You are going to pretend that you are someone else. Here are some suggestions as to who you might be: a person you hate, your best friend, a famous person you admire, someone in your family, your teacher. Try to imagine yourself inside this person's head, thinking and feeling the way he or she does. Then, write a description of yourself as this person: how you look, think, feel, what you like and dislike, what makes you happy, what makes you sad, what it's like to wake up in the morning and be you. You might tell your secret wishes and dreams.

FRACTURED FAIRY TALES

TEACHER'S DIRECTIONS: We all know the usual versions of fairy tales such as *Cinderella, Little Red Riding Hood, Snow White, The Three Bears*, etc. You're going to write your own version of one of these tales. For example, in *Little Red Riding Hood*, you could make the wolf the good guy, and Red might be up to some sort of mischief. Or, in *The Three Bears*, Goldilocks could be a spy sent to bring back important information about the Bears. Your story might be a mystery, or funny, or it might take place on Mars. Just imagine, for example, that one of Cinderella's wicked stepsisters has the same size feet as poor Cinderella and the glass slipper fits the stepsister perfectly! Now, make up your own fractured fairy tale.

A PRETEND VISIT

TEACHER'S DIRECTIONS: Wouldn't it be exciting if you could visit a famous person, living or dead, or a fictional character from a book that you've enjoyed? You're going to have the chance to describe that scene now. Pretend that you are visiting the president of the United States, or Christopher Columbus, or John Lennon, or Oliver Twist, or your favorite actor or actress. You may choose anyone, living or dead, real or fictional. Write about your visit: where it takes place, how your visitor looks, what's said and done, etc.

AN ANIMAL STORY: Children of all ages love animals and enjoy personifying them. Before asking the students to write their own animal stories, it might be helpful to read some excerpts from Aesop or Kipling's *Just So Stories*. TEACHER'S DIRECTIONS: Do you know what animals feel like, how they think, what they would like to say if they could? Today, you're going to write an animal story from the point of view of animals. First, decide what animals you will write about, pets or wild creatures. Your characters can be big, like elephants, or small, like turtles, or a combination of sizes and types. Will your story take place in a zoo, a jungle, a forest, or an ordinary home? Have several animal characters in your story. Pretend that they can talk to each other. What will they say? What will they do?

PROBLEM STORIES: Students of all ages enjoy writing about characters who have problems similar to their own. A fifth-grader might choose to describe buddies whose friendship is threatened by a third party. A sixth-grade boy who loves football might enjoy describing a fictional game over which he, as writer, has complete control. Seventh- and eighth-graders (particularly girls) like writing about boy and girl situations and romance. Eighth-graders may get into more intense situations such as divorce, peer pressure, etc. Often, it can be a release for youngsters to write about their own problems. Fictionalizing them makes them safer.

TEACHER'S INSTRUCTIONS: Tommy is Mike's best friend. They used to spend all their free time together. Lately, Mike has been playing with Kevin a lot. He doesn't have much time for Tommy anymore. Has this, or something like it, ever happened to you or to someone you know? You can make up a story about people who have this problem or any other problem you can think of. It can be a problem with friends, a problem at home like a bossy older sister, a difficulty at school, or any other problem you might wish to write about. Start with your main character. Describe him or her. Tell about the problem and the other people involved. Tell what happens. Your story could have a happy ending or a sad ending. It's up to you.

DEVELOPING A STORY FROM A MORAL OR ADAGE: A well-known adage or moral can be used to stimulate creative writing. Tell the students to make up a story that illustrates one of the adages listed on the chalkboard or on a lesson sheet. Here are some possibilities:

> Honesty is the best policy.
> A stitch in time saves nine.
> Don't put off till tomorrow what you can do today.
> Don't count your chickens before they are hatched.
> The love of money is the root of all evil.
> A bird in hand is worth two in the bush.
> Birds of a feather flock together.
> One man's meat is another man's poison.

Tell the students to make up a story that illustrates one of these adages. When completed, these are usually fun to share with the class by reading aloud.

THE HERO/HEROINE

. In real life, you may be an ordinary kid, but as a writer, you have the power to make yourself brilliant, good-looking, strong, brave, and kind. Just answer the questions on this Worksheet. You will see how easy it is!

1. What is your hero/heroine's name and age? (Use your own first name, but you don't have to be truthful about age.)_____

   _____

2. Describe your hero/heroine's appearance: height, build, coloring, hair, eyes, etc. (You can exaggerate here as much as you like.)_____

   _____

   _____

   _____

   _____

3. Where does your hero/heroine live: home, town, city, country, planet, etc.? (You don't have to be truthful.)

   _____

   _____

   _____

4. Describe his/her intelligence and abilities. (Use your imagination!)_____

   _____

   _____

   _____

5. Write one or two paragraphs using the information above. Pretend it is the beginning of a story and you are introducing your hero. Begin with his/her name and age. (You can continue on the back of this sheet.)

   _____

   _____

   _____

   _____

   _____

   _____

   _____

Name_____   Date_____

WHAT IF?

1. Summarize your "What If" idea briefly by completing the following sentence: WHAT IF_____

   _____

   _____

   _____

   _____

2. Where does this story take place?_____

   _____

3. When (year, month)?_____

   Write your story below. First introduce your main character (use your description of a hero/heroine). Then, tell where and when this is happening. This is just a first draft, so don't worry about handwriting, grammar, spelling, etc. Just get your story down on paper! Have fun! Write the title here (if you have one):_____

   _____

   _____

   _____

   _____

   _____

   _____

   _____

   _____

   _____

   _____

   _____

   _____

   _____

(Use the back of this paper if you need more room.)

Name_____   Date_____

CREATING A NEW WORLD

(GRADES 4 AND 5)

THE TOWN OF…

Would you like to be able to create a town or city exactly the way you want it? As a writer, you have that power. You're going to use your imagination to write a story about a place where you make all the rules.

First, you must decide on a name for your town. You could call it by the name of the real town or city in which you live, or you can make up a name. Here are some names which other boys and girls have used: *Happytown, USA, The City of Water, Animal Land, Dance Town, Sportsland, Football City, Yukville,* and *Playtown.* You may use one of these names, or make up one of your own.

Then, tell all about your town. Is it big or little? What does it look like? What kind of buildings are there? Who lives in this town? What do they look like? How do they dress? What do they eat?

What kind of houses do the people live in? What time do they get up in the morning and go to sleep at night? (Perhaps they sleep during the day and get up at night?) What do they do all day?

Are there stores in the town? Describe them. What are the schools like? Who's in charge?

Your town can be serious or silly. It can be beautiful or disgusting or scary. It can be peaceful or violent.

It's up to you!

(Begin your first draft below; then continue on a separate page.)

Mushroom Village

Hello my name is fatima and I
live in a small village called Mushroom
village, where All the people live in
Mushroom cottages. It is a very peaceful
village and there is a small stream, where
the people get their water. There is an
orchard where the people get the food.
The people who live there are like
humans but smaller. All of my family
members live there. This village is in
kind of like a place similar to a meadow but where there
is water. There is nobody in charge. If
there is any trouble between the people

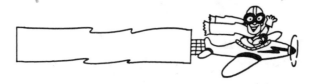

(2-3A)

the one who started it gets
Kicked out and can never come
back in because there is a magical
force field. It. is a very beutiful
village.

Rough
Draft .

Name_____ Date_____

CREATING A NEW WORLD

(GRADES 6, 7, AND 8)

THE LAND OF...

A writer has the power to create things just the way he or she wishes them to be. A writer's imagination is not limited by the rules of the real world.

You are going to create your own country, where you alone make all the rules. It can exist anywhere on the Earth or on another planet. First, you must think of a name for your nation, and use it as part of your title, *The Land of...* Here are some names other writers have used: *Rock and Roll Land, Hockeymania, The Land of Water, Cartoonland, Computerland, Danceland.* You can use one of these or make up your own name.

Tell all about your country and its inhabitants. Describe what your land looks like—size, shape, mountains, rivers, oceans, climate, etc. Describe the people who live there—what they look like, how they dress, what they eat, etc. Tell about the cities in which they live—size, names, kinds of buildings. Describe the lifestyle of your people—how families live, their houses and furnishings, jobs, schools, hobbies, pets, and playthings. What kinds of music, books, and art do they have?

How do your people communicate—language, books, newspapers, TV, movies, etc.? What kind of government do they have? What laws must they obey? Who makes these laws? Who enforces them? Who rules, and how?

Use lots of detail and description—the more the better!

Write notes below, and begin your first draft on a separate paper.

_____

_____

_____

_____

_____

_____

_____

_____

_____

_____

_____

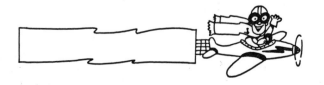

PLACE DESCRIPTION:
SENSORY WORDS

When you write a description, you are painting a word picture. Sensory words are a big help in making your description alive to the reader. Just to get you in the right mood, write some sensory words in the spaces below. Write three words or phrases that tell how something looks.

_____

Write three words that tell how something sounds.

_____

Write three words that tell how something smells.

_____

Write three words that tell how something feels.

_____

Write three words that tell how something tastes.

_____

Following is a description that your teacher has read to you. Underline all the sensory words in this description.

> The rose garden was a sweet-smelling enclosure far out on the rear grounds. The circular garden was formed by the bushes—a round tangle of roses of every type and color. There were climbers and ramblers and tea roses—reds, pinks, yellows, and whites. In the center was a grassy clearing, completely hidden from the house by the tight knot of thorny bushes. There was a white wrought-iron bench on the grass, decorated with carvings of roses. Jennie felt more comfortable here than anywhere else. There was a sort of warmth about the spot.

PLACE DESCRIPTION:
CHOOSING A PLACE

Now it's time to choose a subject for your own description. Choose something that you know well, that you can see clearly in your mind. It can be a real place, or one that exists only in your imagination. Here are some possibilities:

• your room at home

• a place that is scary or mysterious

• your classroom

• the street on which you live

• a place where you feel happy

• a park you've often visited

• the inside of your locker

• a place you've seen in your dreams

• the lunchroom at school

• a store or restaurant near your home

You should choose a place that you remember in great detail. Try to picture this place in your mind. Use all of your senses in remembering this place. Think about what you see, hear, feel, taste, or smell. On the lines below, list places you could describe. You may include suggestions from above.

_____

_____

_____

_____

_____

Now choose one place you would most like to describe:

_____

_____

_____

_____

_____

_____

PLACE DESCRIPTION:
BRAINSTORMING

Before you try to organize the picture in your mind into a written form, it is helpful to do some brainstorming. *Brainstorming* just means that you will jot down a list of ideas. The more ideas and details you include in your list, the easier it will be for you to write your description.

The person who wrote the description of the rose garden might have had a brainstorming list like this:

    sweet-smelling garden
    bushes arranged in a circle
    kinds of roses: tea roses, climbers, ramblers
    colors: red, pink, yellow, white
    grassy clearing in center
    white, wrought-iron bench, with carvings, on grass
    clearing hidden from house

Begin your brainstorming list below. Write down the name of your subject on the first line. Then, write as many details as possible. Show your list to the teacher before beginning your description.

_____

_____

_____

_____

_____

_____

_____

Now write the first draft of your description on a separate paper. Include all the details on your brainstorming list. Use sensory images where possible.

_____

_____

_____

_____

_____

_____

_____

WRITING A DESCRIPTION OF A PERSON

When you write about a person, either real or imagined, you can probably see that person in your mind. You know whether he or she is tall or short, fat, slim, or muscular. You can see that person's hair and eyes, the way he or she smiles, speaks, and moves. Perhaps you can even hear the sound of his or her voice in your mind.

Your reader does not know any of these things unless you describe them. The reader can only visualize the person as painted by the words and phrases you use. That's why it is important, in a description, to write down every detail, no matter how small. Even the shape of a hand, or a habit of running fingers through hair, will make your portrait come alive to the reader.

You're going to write a paragraph (or more, if you wish) describing someone who is well known, someone everyone in the class will be able to identify, perhaps an actor, politician, rock star, TV personality, etc., but you're not going to write down his or her name. When everyone has finished writing a description, each student will read his or hers aloud. Then the rest of the class will try to identify the person being described. If your description is good, the identity of your subject should be quite clear. On the lines below, write names of possible subjects. Circle the one you would most like to describe, *BUT DO NOT SHOW IT TO ANYONE EXCEPT THE TEACHER.*

_____

_____

_____

_____

_____

_____

_____

_____

_____

_____

_____

_____

_____

PERSONAL DESCRIPTION:
BRAINSTORMING LIST

PART ONE: Write as many words and phrases as you can think of that describe your subject's face and head. (Examples: blue-eyed, curly hair, blonde, clear-skinned, full cheeks, pug nose, etc.):

PART TWO: Write as many words and phrases as you can think of that describe your subject's body. (Examples: tall, skinny, tiny, large-boned, muscular, etc.):

PART THREE: Write as many words and phrases as you can think of that describe your subject's way of walking. (Examples: tiny steps, strides, runs swiftly, etc.):

PART FOUR: Write phrases that describe your subject's mannerisms. (Examples: smiles a lot, blinks rapidly, bites his nails, etc.)

PART FIVE: Write phrases that describe your subject's way of talking. (Example: talks fast, slurs words, uses big words, squeaky voice, roars like a lion, etc.):

PART SIX: Write as many words and phrases as you can think of that describe your subject's personality. (Examples: unfriendly, sociable, kind, gentle, mean, quick to fight, etc.)

Now, write your description on a separate sheet of paper. Use details from your brainstorming lists. Try to make your word picture so real that your classmates will have no trouble identifying the subject.

Name_____ Date_____

FILL-IN STORY: YOUNG TOM TURKEY

DIRECTIONS: Write your own words or phrases in the blanks below. Then complete the story.

All the turkeys in the _____ were acting strangely. They were running about in a _____ manner and had very _____ looks on their _____ faces.

Young Tom Turkey didn't know what was going on. He was _____ confused. He went to find his mother. Mrs. Turkey was in the _____, cooking _____.

"Why is everyone acting so _____?" Tom asked.

"I'm too _____ to talk to you now," said Mrs. Turkey in a _____ voice. "Go ask your father."

Mr. Turkey was in the _____. He was _____ his _____. "Why are all the turkeys so _____?" asked Tom.

"Don't bother me now, son," said Mr. Turkey in a _____ voice. "I have to finish this _____. Go ask the Old Sage."

The Old Sage was an ancient turkey. He was as old as _____. He knew more about _____ than any other turkey on the _____. Tom found Old Sage behind the _____. He was standing on top of a _____, and scratching his _____. "You're looking very _____, Tom," he said.

"Old Sage," asked Tom in a _____ voice. "Why are the turkeys acting so _____ today?"

Old Sage _____ his _____ eyes. "Don't you know that tomorrow is Thanksgiving?"

Tom's eyes _____. "What's Thanksgiving?" he asked.

"Thanksgiving is the _____ day of the year for turkeys," said Old Sage.

"Why, what happens?" _____ Tom.

"I can't tell you the _____ details," said Old Sage. "They're far too _____ and _____ for your _____ ears. Just remember that you soon must hide."

Tom began to feel _____. "Where should I hide?"

"Find a place that's _____ and _____," advised Old Sage. "Do it now."

Tom was getting more _____ by the minute. He looked all around for a place to hide. He found a spot behind the _____. Poor Tom's _____ was shaking. Suddenly, he heard a _____ noise. In the blanks below, finish the story in your own words. Use the back of this paper if you need more room.)

_____

_____

_____

FILL-IN STORY: A SCARY HALLOWEEN

DIRECTIONS: Fill in the blanks below with your own words and phrases. Then complete the story.

It was a dark and _____ Halloween night. Patrick and his _____ friend, Zach, were out trick-or-treating. Patrick was wearing a _____ costume. Zach was dressed as a _____. They had already gone to _____ houses. They had collected lots of _____ for their _____ bags. They came to the _____ house at the _____ end of _____ Street.

"I don't want to go to that _____ house," said Zach. "It's too _____."

"C'mon," insisted Patrick. "Don't be such a _____." Patrick walked up the _____ path. Zach followed _____ behind. They came to the _____ door. It was _____ and _____. On the door was hanging a _____. Above the doorbell was a sign that read, "_____."

"Let's _____," said Zach in a _____ voice.

But Patrick rang the _____ bell. A _____ sound filled the air.

"Let's go," begged Zach. "This place is too _____."

At that moment, the door opened with a _____ sound. A _____old woman appeared. Her hair was _____ and _____. Her eyes were like _____. Her nose was shaped like a _____. She was wearing a long _____. On her head was a _____. "What do you want?" she asked in a _____ voice.

Zach was too _____ to talk. Patrick managed to say, "_____."

The woman's _____ eyes _____ like _____. "I'll give you _____ kids a fine _____," she said in a voice like a _____. She held out one of her _____ hands. In it was _____. (In the blanks below, finish the story in your own words. Use the back of this paper if you need more room.)

_____

_____

_____

_____

_____

_____

_____

_____

_____

Name_____   Date_____

FILL-IN STORY: THE LAST CLASS

DIRECTIONS: Write your own words or phrases in the blanks below. Then complete the story.

It was the last _____ class on the last day before summer vacation. Rachel was seated at her desk in the _____ row, thinking about all the _____ things she would do during the summer. She was planning to _____ with her friends. She also wanted to _____ and to go to _____. Later, in _____, she was going with her family to _____.

The teacher, Mrs. _____, was talking, but no one was listening. While Rachel was dreaming about _____, her friend, _____, who sat in the _____ row, was _____ on her desk. Timmy _____, who sat behind Rachel, was _____ a _____ with the kid next to him. On the other _____ of the room, Jason was throwing _____. Other kids were tossing _____ around.

Mrs. _____ looked very _____. "Stop throwing those _____," she _____ in a _____ voice. She was a _____ woman with _____ hair and a _____ manner. The kids _____ her. Jason got up and began to _____. Timmy tacked a _____ on _____.

Mrs. _____ looked as if she was going to _____. "You'd better _____," she said in a _____ voice. "Or I'll keep the _____ after school."

At that, _____ sat down. The other _____ students stopped _____ around. The _____ noise became _____.

"That's _____ better," said Mrs. _____ in a _____ voice. Then she pointed to the _____ clock on the _____ wall. "Look," she exclaimed. "It's _____ o'clock!"

Everyone looked at the _____ clock. The students began to _____, and ...(In the blanks below, finish the story in your own words. Use the back of this paper if you need more room.)

_____

_____

_____

_____

_____

A DAY IN THE LIFE OF

PART ONE—BRAINSTORMING: Write a list of all the things your subject does, where he/she/it goes, and what he/she/it does from early in the morning until late at night. Don't go into detail on this list—just jot down each event briefly.

_____

_____

_____

_____

_____

_____

_____

_____

_____

_____

_____

_____

_____

_____

_____

_____

_____

_____

_____

PART TWO—WRITING YOUR STORY: Describe a whole day in the life of your subject, using your brainstorming list as a guide. Give lots of detail. Adjectives and sensory words will help bring your story to life. You will probably find it easiest to begin by describing your subject. Write your first draft on a separate sheet of paper.

WRITING TO A PICTURE

DIRECTIONS: You are going to write a story based on a picture. Examine the picture carefully. Don't just glance at it, but really study all the details before you begin to write. Think about what might be happening. You are not going to describe just what you see in the picture. You are going to make up a story based on this picture. You will find it a great help to complete the brainstorming exercises before beginning the actual story.

BRAINSTORMING: Answer the questions in the space provided, using *as many details as possible*.

WHO ARE THESE PEOPLE? Write something about every person in the picture. Tell how old they are, what their personalities are like. Are they related in any way to the other people in the picture? What are they thinking or saying at the moment of the picture? Do this for each person pictured.

WHERE AND WHEN IS THIS SCENE TAKING PLACE? What town, what country, what planet, what day, what year? List the details that support this decision.

WHAT IS HAPPENING IN THIS SCENE? Why are these particular people in this particular place? What is each doing and saying at this moment? Why?

WHAT HAPPENED BEFORE THIS? Describe all past events that led up to the moment in this scene. What happened yesterday or last week or ten years ago to bring these people together at this time?

WHAT IS GOING TO HAPPEN NEXT? What will happen after this? What is each person going to do next? Why? Where will they go? Why? How will their story end? Why?

Now you are ready to begin your story (on a separate paper). Write it as though no one else but you has seen this picture. Use lots of details and sensory words to describe your characters and the action. Try to make the story exciting and suspenseful.

3
WRITING A PERSONAL ESSAY

Students are often turned off by the word *essay*. It smacks of English and social studies homework, and carries with it connotations such as "dull," "heavy," or "sleep-inducing." It is the exceptional student who looks on an essay assignment as a challenge, even, possibly, as fun. These are usually the students who have a facility in writing. Even when the topic is interesting, perhaps exciting, average students are so threatened by the necessity of putting their thoughts into organized, written form that they become resistant. Their negativity keeps them from enjoying the exhilaration that a confident, creative approach would bring.

The process writing system, when applied to essay writing, can help students reach a level of skill in organization and composition that will give them confidence to approach these assignments in a more positive manner. It is, therefore, vital for you to lead the students through the steps of the process method for the projects in this chapter. *Brainstorming* is a proven way for students to marshall their thoughts, facts, and ideas and discover the benefits of organization. *Peer critiquing* shows writers the gaps and distortions in their manuscripts, and where they have failed to communicate effectively their message to readers. Spotting the flaws in the work of other writers sharpens students' skills in locating their own. To assist in this critiquing process, an evaluation ("Group Response") Worksheet is included that can be used effectively in all essay activities that include group critiquing to focus responses and provide information for the author.

In this chapter, most of the actual student writing will be in the category of personal essay. No research is required for most of these projects, and their personal nature, arising from the writers' own experiences, feelings, and ideas, will help students attain a feeling of competence quickly. In any activity where facts usually obtained through research are needed, these will be supplied in the Worksheet.

Activity 1   THE THINK TANK

Seasoned writers usually spend much time mulling over a project before putting pen to paper (or, to update this image, fingers to computer keyboard). They don't plunge into writing the moment an idea occurs to them. Once the seed has been planted, they let it germinate, reaching out with their minds to touch ideas, letting some drop and holding on to others. This process may take only a brief time measured in hours, in which case the level of concentration is probably exceedingly intense, or it can take days, even weeks of occasional mental meanderings.

This is one form of brainstorming. Unlike the goddess Athena, most productions do not spring out, perfect and fully formed, from the heads of their creators. They must be carefully thought out and organized. While experienced writers can sometimes do this in their minds, most students cannot. For them to become skilled in the art of brainstorming, which is a necessary prerequisite to a well-thought-out essay, they must write their ideas down on paper. This project will provide guided practice in the techniques of brainstorming.

PREWRITING ACTIVITIES

1. Write the words *Think Tank* on the chalkboard. Ask the students if they know what this is. Some of the older students may be able to define the term. Younger students probably will not. If no one in the class comes up with an answer, tell them that a think tank is a sort of laboratory—a collection of minds, where people use their combined brain power to come up with ideas or answers to problems that none of them could solve alone.

2. Write the name of your school on the chalkboard in front of *Think Tank* (for example, *Glenview Middle School Think Tank*). Tell the students that for the remainder of the class period, this room is being transformed into a think tank.

3. Write on the chalkboard: *School Cafeteria*. Ask the students to suggest any facts, opinions, words, or phrases that have anything at all to do with the school cafeteria. (If there is no cafeteria or lunchroom in your school, choose another topic, preferably one with which the students have daily contact.) Write all the students' suggestions—no matter how outrageous— on the chalkboard. You will probably end up with a long list.

4. Tell the students they have just done the first step in writing an essay—brainstorming. Elicit from them the fact that in order to produce an essay, they must organize the ideas and details they have just come up with. Ask them to suggest headings under which this material could be organized. They will produce several ideas. Choose the simplest one, which will probably be *What's Good about the Cafeteria, What's Bad about the Cafeteria,* and *What Could Be Done to Improve the Cafeteria*. Begin three columns on the chalkboard with this heading. Ask the students to divide the items on their first list into these three categories. Write the items on the chalkboard in the appropriate category.

5. Ask the students how they would use this material to compose an essay. It will be clear to at least some students that their essays might begin with a description of the good aspects of the school cafeteria, followed by a discussion of the negative things, ending with suggestions for improvement and the writer's conclusion. There are, of course, many other possible arrangements.

6. Distribute Worksheet 3-1A THINK TANK. Read the directions for each part together. After each part, have the students read their lists aloud. Tell the students to augment their own lists with the contributions of the others.

7. Distribute Worksheet 3-1B MORE THINK TANK. Follow same procedure as in item 6.

8. Distribute Worksheet 3-1C THE IDEA TREE. Read directions, and guide the students through the various sections of this Worksheet, which offers a kind of clustering exercise.

NOTE: Be certain the students understand that these activities require only *lists, not* completed essays.

Activity 2   NARRATIVE WRITING ─────────────────

In this exercise, the students will prepare a brainstorming list, organize their material, and use these notes to write an essay. Since most of us can write more fluently about our own lives and experiences, this essay will be in the form of a personal narrative.

PREWRITING ACTIVITIES

1. Read the following short narrative (also found on Worksheet 3-2A) aloud to the class.

I'll never forget our first afternoon in Florida. We had just arrived in Fort Lauderdale, and were in the hotel room unpacking. It was a large, bright room, with two double beds, two elegant dressers painted gold and white, a matching desk and chair, and, best of all, a large color TV. My brother, Frank, who is a real couch potato, immediately flicked on the TV. One of his favorite movies, *The Fly*, was on. Frank flopped down on the bed and began to enjoy the film. I was curious, since I had never seen that movie, so I watched, too.

Our parents made us go out. "We're paying lots of money for all this sunshine and ocean," they pointed out, "so you'd better enjoy it."

Frank and I put on our bathing suits and went out on the beach. We swam in the ocean and walked around a little and then got bored. Besides, they were going to repeat the showing of *The Fly*. So we went back up to the room. The movie was great, but Mom and Dad weren't too happy. That was how our whole week there went—Frank and me trying to watch TV; Mom and Dad pushing us out.

2. Let the class decide on a title for this essay. Discuss the characteristics of a good personal narrative, such as a detailed description of surroundings and events that make the readers feel they are there, a sharing of feelings that help the readers identify with the narrator, and perhaps a bit of dialogue for variety. Point out how the writer of the preceding essay focused on one aspect of the experience instead of trying to cover the entire trip.

3. Distribute Worksheet 3-2A SELECTING AND FOCUSING. Read the directions for Part One—Making Choices. When Part One has been completed, share and discuss results. Do the same for Part Two.

4. Distribute Worksheet 3-2B WRITING A PERSONAL ESSAY. Read the directions aloud. Instruct students to show their brainstorming lists and organizations to you before beginning the first draft.

5. Complete the first draft of the personal essay. Then go through all the steps of process writing—group critiquing, revisions, etc. You can use the GROUP RESPONSE Worksheet 3-1 for the peer critiquing portion of the process.

Activity 3   ANOTHER PERSONAL ESSAY

This project utilizes brainstorming techniques and an abbreviated version of the process writing method. It omits peer group critiquing and can, therefore, be used when there is less time.

PREWRITING ACTIVITIES

1. Review brainstorming, including organization of items into subject lists.

2. Discuss or review the benefits of using strong, active verbs instead of passive, weak ones. Write examples on the chalkboard (i.e., *run* or *stroll* instead of *go; stare* or *examine* instead of *see; shout* or *moan* instead of *speak*; etc.). Ask the students to add to these lists.

3. Discuss or review the use of words that appeal to the senses. Elicit examples of sensory words, and write them on the chalkboard under the headings "Taste," "Smell," "Touch," "Sound," "Sight."

4. Discuss or review similes and metaphors. Elicit several examples of each, and write them on the chalkboard.

NOTE: If it is not appropriate for the class to discuss or review active verbs, sensory words, similes, or metaphors, any or all of items 2, 3, and 4 may be omitted. In that event, the corresponding directions on the Worksheet can be ignored.

5. Distribute Worksheet 3-3 ANOTHER PERSONAL ESSAY. Read the directions aloud. Depending on the abilities of the students in the class, you may wish to do one step at a time, or read and discuss all directions before beginning to write. It is usually a good idea to stress the suggestions under "Step Five" (writing the first draft) to encourage ease in writing this draft.

Activity 4   ONE, TWO, THREE! ━━━━━━━━━━━━━━━━━━

This project can be used for students or classes who are having trouble writing their essays even after practice in brainstorming. Brainstorming and organizational lists are of immense help to students, and usually prepare them to approach the actual writing of an essay with confidence. Some individuals and/or groups, however, can master the techniques of brainstorming and listmaking, and still experience difficulty when the time comes to set down their thoughts in paragraph form. This essay and basic exercise teaches paragraphing as it applies to essay writing.

PREWRITING ACTIVITIES

1. Tell the students that they are going to learn a trick that will make essay writing a snap.

2. Distribute Worksheet 3-4 ONE, TWO, THREE! Read aloud the directions at the top of the Worksheet. Discuss topics listed on the Worksheet that lend themselves to being divided into three parts. Write some additional topics on the chalkboard. Tell the students to choose a topic and complete the title line on the Worksheet.

3. Read Worksheet directions for the first paragraph, and give an example, such as: "My three best friends are Tony, Eric, and Scott. I spend most of my free time with one or more of them. Sometimes we all hang out together." Then, have students complete the section for their first paragraph on the Worksheet.

4. Read Worksheet directions for the second paragraph, and give an example, such as: "My first friend is Tony. He is my oldest pal. I've known him since I was three. We started preschool together." Then, have students complete the section for their second paragraph on the Worksheet.

5. Do the same for paragraphs three, four, and five. (Paragraph three will tell about Eric. Paragraph four will describe Scott. Paragraph five will sum up, i.e., "These are my three friends. I can't imagine life without them. I hope we will be buddies all our lives.")

6. The students can now write their essays on a separate piece of paper, copying what is on the Worksheet and adding further details.

Activity 5   BEGINNINGS AND ENDINGS ━━━━━━━━━━━━━━

"My way is to begin with the beginning." Easy enough for Lord Byron to say, with his literary gifts! Student writers, however, often find that getting started is the biggest stumbling block. Brainstorming lists are great for providing a concrete reservoir of ideas for content, but plucking a beginning from that ocean of words can be perplexing.

Once started, the central section, the meat of the essay, can be quite easily accomplished, but how to end that middle portion and lead it into the conclusion may provide another challenge. Whole chapters can be written on how to introduce and conclude essays. Here, we offer a few Worksheets to reinforce the techniques for beginning and ending essays.

PREWRITING ACTIVITIES

1. Ask the students how many of them sometimes find it difficult to get started with an essay. Almost every hand will go up.

2. Distribute Worksheet 3-5A DYNAMITE BEGINNINGS. Read Part One—Samples. Discuss the various types of introductions that are mentioned.

3. Read and discuss directions for Part Two—Try It Yourself. Emphasize that the students should use each of the three types of beginnings shown in the samples. Be sure they understand that they are going to write just the introductory paragraph, not a complete essay.

4. When the students have completed Part Two of the Worksheet, share and discuss the results. Do some types of beginnings work better than others? What makes one kind easier to use than another? What makes one more effective than another?

5. Distribute Worksheet 3-5B WRAPPING IT UP. Read and discuss Part One—Samples.

6. Read and discuss directions for Part Two—Try It Yourself.

7. When the students have completed Part Two of the Worksheet, share and discuss the results.

Activity 6   ASK THE EXPERT

Everyone, even a child, has some area of expertise—some subject or activity he or she knows more about than most. These areas of expertise could be the result of hobbies, reading, family activities or conversations, experiences, etc. This project encourages students to share their knowledge with others. It is also a good way to promote writing skills, because knowledge of a topic creates self-confidence, and this self-confidence will carry over into the writing experience.

PREWRITING ACTIVITIES

1. Distribute Worksheet 3-6 ASK THE EXPERT. Read the directions for Part One aloud. Instruct the students to list any subjects they feel they know more about than many people their age. Confer individually with students who fail to come up with anything. Encourage them to think about after-school activities, hobbies, pets, cooking, or repairing they may help out with at home, subjects about which they may have read more than one book or article, items they may have spent a lot of time shopping for, etc.

2. Read aloud Worksheet instructions for brainstorming. Have students show you their brainstorming lists before beginning a first draft.

3. When the first draft has been completed, follow process writing steps.

Activity 7   MAKING CHANGES

"Progress is impossible without change," wrote George Bernard Shaw, "and those who cannot change their minds cannot change anything."

Young people often have the desire to alter many things in their lives and environment, but they lack the power to effect such changes. In this project, they will be shown how the written expression of their complaints and remedies may not only make them feel better (the proverbial "getting things off one's chest"), but may sometimes actually cause others to change their minds, beginning a process that may make their wishes come true. This can only be accomplished if student-writers examine their ideas, then organize and present them in a clear, persuasive manner. This project will help give young writers the tools and experience to bring about change through written expression.

PREWRITING ACTIVITIES

1. Write the following sentence on the chalkboard: *The pen is mightier than the sword.* Elicit the meaning of this adage through class discussion.

2. Ask the students to give examples of writings that have brought about change. If they look at you blankly, suggest that they think about early U.S. history. They might then be able to come up with the Declaration of Independence, the writings of Thomas Jefferson, Benjamin Franklin, Thomas Paine, etc. Other examples they offer (with teacher guidance, if necessary) might be the Bible, *Uncle Tom's Cabin*, the newspaper exposés that led to Watergate, etc. You might tell them how the novels of Charles Dickens were instrumental in bringing about child protection laws in England. (Some students may be familiar with *Oliver Twist* from the movie *Oliver!*)

3. Ask the students if there are any things in their own lives they would like to change. Tell them that these could be as simple as what their parents make them eat for dinner, or the nature of homework assignments. Write their suggestions on the chalkboard.

4. Distribute Worksheet 3-7A MAKING CHANGES. Read aloud the directions for Part One and Part Two. Have students show you their lists before going on to Part Three.

5. Use the process writing steps of drafts, critiquing, and revising for this project.

6. Follow the same procedures for Worksheet 3-7B MAKING BIGGER CHANGES.

Activity 8 WHAT DO YOU THINK?

After students have had some experience in essay writing and have mastered the techniques of brainstorming, organizing material, and going through the revising and critiquing steps of the process method, they will enjoy some activities that can be done more quickly and effortlessly.

These projects omit written brainstorming lists and process writing steps. The resultant essays may not be as polished or excellent as the final copies of previous activities. If, however, the students have already had some grounding in using these writing tools, their essays may turn out surprisingly well. Without realizing it themselves, they will probably have internalized these brainstorming and organizing activities, and continue to use them, albeit only in their heads. These shorter projects can serve as reinforcement in essay writing when there is less class time available.

This project is particularly helpful with reluctant writers. Most of them will have strong opinions about the subject. Also, the class discussions before writing will provide stimulation and a source of ready-to-use ideas.

PREWRITING ACTIVITIES

1. Write on the chalkboard the three statements offered in Worksheet 3-8A WHAT DO YOU THINK?:

Boys are better than girls in every way.
Homework is a waste of time.
It's better to have one good friend than be part of a group.

2. Ask students to indicate by a show of hands whether they agree or disagree with the first statement. Initiate a discussion of the topic by asking for their reasons. Do the same for each of the other statements.

3. Distribute Worksheet 3-8A WHAT DO YOU THINK? Read the directions aloud. Suggest that the students spend some time thinking about their arguments. If they wish to prepare a written brainstorming list on a separate paper, they may do so, but it is not necessary.

4. After essays have been completed, share them by having students read them aloud. Group the readings by the topics the writers have chosen.

5. Follow the same procedures for Worksheet 3-8B WHAT DO YOU THINK?

Activity 9   EXPANDING AN IDEA

This activity is especially helpful for students who have trouble turning an idea into a complete essay. It provides them not only with a topic, but also with a ready-made brainstorming list of words and/or phrases. The students are, therefore, relieved from having to cope with one step of the essay-writing process. It is already done for them. This procedure does not restrict initiative, since the lists the students are given are open-ended and can be added to. Although students all start off with the same topic and list of words, the final essays will vary greatly according to the writer's knowledge, ability, and creativity. Most students will enjoy the puzzle-solving aspect of taking the words they are given and organizing them into an essay.

This activity is particularly useful when you want the students to work primarily on their own. The Worksheets are self-explanatory and the directions easy to understand and follow. A minimum of introduction and teacher supervision is required. You might schedule this activity for a day when you wish to do other work with individual students, or when a substitute teacher will be in charge.

PREWRITING ACTIVITIES

1. Distribute Worksheet 3-9A EXPANDING AN IDEA. Tell the students that this type of Worksheet will help them write an essay even on subjects they may not know too much about.

2. The students should be able to follow the directions on their own. You may read and discuss them with younger groups, if necessary.

3. When the first draft has been completed, follow all the critiquing and revising steps of the process method.

4. Follow the same procedures for Worksheet 3-9B EXPANDING AN IDEA.

Name_____ Date_____

GROUP RESPONSE WORKSHEET

I read "_____," by _____

   1. What is the focus of this essay?

_____

_____

_____

_____

   2. Good things about this essay:

_____

_____

_____

_____

   3. Are there any parts that aren't clear? What are they?

_____

_____

_____

_____

   4. Questions for author:

_____

_____

_____

_____

   5. Suggestions for author:

_____

_____

_____

_____

THINK TANK

PART ONE—BRAINSTORMING LIST

DIRECTIONS: Prepare a brainstorming list for an essay titled "Saturday Afternoon at the Mall." Write down all the words, phrases, and sentences you can think of describing the sights, activities, people, events, and feelings you would encounter during an afternoon's shopping at a mall.

_____

_____

_____

_____

_____

_____

_____

_____

_____

_____

_____

PART TWO—ORGANIZING

DIRECTIONS: Now, organize your list by rewriting each of the words, phrases, and sentences under the heading that fits best:

STORES/RESTAURANTS   *PEOPLE*   *ACTIVITIES*   *OTHER*

_____

_____

_____

_____

_____

_____

_____

MORE THINK TANK

PART ONE—BRAINSTORMING

DIRECTIONS: Prepare a brainstorming list for an essay titled "A Visit to the Dentist." Write down all the words, phrases, and sentences you can think of.

_____

_____

_____

_____

_____

_____

_____

_____

_____

_____

_____

_____

PART TWO—ORGANIZING

DIRECTIONS: Now, organize the words, phrases, and sentences in your brainstorming list under the appropriate heading below:

PEOPLE   **OFFICE**   **ACTIONS**   **FEELINGS**

_____

_____

_____

_____

_____

_____

THE IDEA TREE

There are other ways to brainstorm, things you can do that will stimulate your mind and help you develop the ideas you will need to write a good essay. Some people say that meditation makes them more creative. Others claim they get great inspiration after exercise, such as jogging.

You can experiment at home with meditation or jogging before you begin your homework. Maybe you'll start getting better grades! This Worksheet concentrates on another interesting technique for getting ideas for essay writing.

PART ONE—THE IDEA TREE: You've probably heard of family trees. Perhaps your own family has one. These are diagrams of family members that cover many generations. Like trees, they have branches that go off in many directions. These branches grow branches of their own, and so forth. The Idea Tree also has branches. These branches are the ideas that are inspired by a word or phrase. Each branch goes in a different direction, giving rise to its own branches. Here is an Idea Tree that starts with the word *future*:

Some branches of this tree grow more detailed than others. You could probably add to some of the branches of this Idea Tree, and soon have more than enough information to write an essay. Can you build Idea Trees from the two words below? (In the first one, some branches are started for you.) Some branches may end after only one word. Others you may wish to continue to build on and on.

sports   music

team sports

baseball

SELECTING AND FOCUSING

Read the following essay:

I'll never forget our first afternoon in Florida. We had just arrived in Fort Lauderdale, and were in the hotel room unpacking. It was a large, bright room, with two double beds, two elegant dressers painted gold and white, a matching desk and chair, and, best of all, a large color TV. My brother, Frank, who is a real couch potato, immediately clicked on the TV. One of his favorite movies, *The Fly*, was on. Frank flopped down on the bed and began to enjoy the film. I was curious, since I had never seen that movie, so I watched, too.

Our parents made us go out. "We're paying lots of money for all this sunshine and ocean," they pointed out, "so you'd better enjoy it."

Frank and I put on our bathing suits and went out on the beach. We swam in the ocean and walked around a little and then got bored. Besides, they were going to repeat the showing of *The Fly*. So, we went back up to the room. The movie was great, but Mom and Dad weren't too happy. That was how our whole week there went—Frank and me trying to watch TV; Mom and Dad pushing us out.

Here is the author's brainstorming list:			
Florida	Fort Lauderdale	airport	plane
takeoff	landing	luggage	taxi
palm trees	hot	crowds	hotel
large room	two double beds	dressers	desk
chair	color TV	Mom	Dad
Frank	favorite movie	"The Fly"	watch
parents made us go out		cost of vacation	
"You'd better enjoy it!"		beach	ocean
swimsuits	waves	sand	swim
beachball	kids on beach	sunburn	sweaty
boats	sand castles	helicopters	boring
great movies	Mom and Dad		
	angry	one week	more TV

PART ONE—MAKING CHOICES: In his essay, the writer used some, but not all, of the ideas on his brainstorming list. Circle those that were used in the essay.

PART TWO: Answer the following questions.

1. What part of the vacation did the writer focus on?

_____

2. Why didn't the writer include all the words on the list?

_____

3. How did the writer feel about Florida? How does he let you know that?

_____

Name_____   Date_____

WRITING A PERSONAL ESSAY

DIRECTIONS: When you write a personal essay, you want your readers to see what happened through your eyes and to share your feelings. It is important to write about something that you remember well. Here are two suggestions:

1. The first time you did something (such as flying in an airplane, or going to the circus, or traveling alone, or seeing your new baby sister or brother)

2. Finding (or losing) something important.

Decide on a title for your essay, and write it below.

_____

Now, prepare a brainstorming list for your essay.

_____

_____

_____

_____

_____

_____

_____

Organize your brainstorming list. Decide on several headings, write them below, and then arrange your list under the appropriate headings. Show your lists to the teacher before writing your first draft.

_____

_____

_____

_____

_____

_____

_____

_____

Now, write the first draft of your personal essay on a separate sheet of paper.

Name_____   Date_____

ANOTHER PERSONAL ESSAY

SUGGESTED TOPICS:

> The Person I Want to Be
>
> Me, Ten Years from Now
>
> My Friends and What They Mean to Me
>
> How I'd Like to Change My Life
>
> My Family
>
> Times I've Been Sad
>
> Times I've Been Happy
>
> The Best Summer of My Life

PROCEDURES

STEP ONE • Choose a topic. Write it at the top of this page.

STEP TWO • BRAINSTORMING. On the back of this paper, make a list of ideas for this essay. The longer your list, the easier it will be to write your essay.

STEP THREE • Select and organize the ideas you will use in your essay. Decide on headings. Group together all ideas that are in the same category.

STEP FOUR • Show your brainstorming list to the teacher.

STEP FIVE • Write your first draft. Try to put down the ideas as they come to you. Don't be too concerned about good writing at this point.

STEP SIX • Proofread and edit your draft. Add words that would make your essay more interesting and alive. Take out words that are unnecessary or confusing. Add phrases or sentences that are necessary to make the meaning clearer.

STEP SEVEN • Show your corrected draft to the teacher for final proofreading and editing.

STEP EIGHT • Write your final copy of the essay.

ADDITIONAL SUGGESTIONS

1. Try to use strong, active verbs instead of passive, weak ones.

2. Use sensory words where possible (words that appeal to your sense of taste, smell, touch, sight, or sound).

3. Try to include at least two similes or metaphors.

ONE, TWO, THREE!

DIRECTIONS: You are going to write the simplest kind of essay by choosing a topic that can be broken down into at least three parts. For example, you could write a theme called, "My Three Pets" if you have owned a hamster, a snake, and a cat. "My Three Heroes" could be a theme about any three people you admire. Here are some more ideas: "My Three Favorite Books," "My Three Friends," "My Three Hobbies," "My Three Favorite TV Characters." Choose one of these topics or any topic that interests you and can be divided into three parts, and complete the title below:

My Three _____

FIRST PARAGRAPH: Tell what the topic is and list the three items. The first sentence is started for you. Finish it, and then write additional ideas about the main topic that would be appropriate for the first paragraph. (These don't have to be complete sentences.) My three _____

_____

_____

SECOND PARAGRAPH: Begin the second paragraph by identifying your first example. The first sentence is started for you. Finish it, and then add any other details that you can use about this item. (These don't have to be complete sentences at this point.) My first _____

_____

_____

THIRD PARAGRAPH: Do the same as above. My second _____

_____

_____

FOURTH PARAGRAPH: Do the same as above. My third _____

_____

_____

FIFTH PARAGRAPH (concludes the theme): These are my three _____

_____

_____

_____

_____

On a separate sheet of paper, write your essay. Copy the first sentence of each paragraph from this Worksheet. Add the other details, using each in a complete sentence.

DYNAMITE BEGINNINGS

PART ONE—SAMPLES: Grab your readers' attention and tell them what the essay is about. That's what a good introduction does. Clever beginnings are fine, but the easy, tried-and-true methods shown here are also effective.

1. Ask a question, and indicate that you will provide an answer: *"What should I pack?" Most people face this dilemma when planning a vacation. Deciding what to take along for a week at the beach can be as difficult as packing for a month in Europe. There are several easy guidelines that can make packing a cinch.*

2. Simply state your topic: *Most kids in a middle school fit into one of three categories. There is the popular "in" group of jocks, party-givers, and cut-ups. Then, there are the serious, hard-working, "good" students. Last are the "different" ones—the outsiders and nerds.*

3. Say something startling or unusual about the subject: *Green! That's the color many kids become after one taste of the hot dishes offered in our school cafeteria. The sandwiches and salads aren't exactly a diner's delight, but the daily specials are the pits.*

PART TWO—TRY IT YOURSELF: Choose three of the topics below, and write an introductory paragraph for each. Use the question method for one, introduce the second by stating the topic, and begin the third with a startling or unusual statement. Circle the three titles you choose.

How to Lose a Friend
The Best TV Shows of the Season
The Toughest Characters on TV
My Favorite Games
The Best Kind of Pets
What Kind of Allowances Should Kids Get?
A Day at the Mall

BEGINNING 1: _____

_____

_____

_____

BEGINNING 2: _____

_____

_____

_____

BEGINNING 3: _____

_____

_____

_____

WRAPPING IT UP

PART ONE—SAMPLES: Every essay needs an ending. It is a signal that the piece is over. Otherwise, readers will feel as if they have been stranded in the middle. In addition, the ending usually offers a summary or conclusion. The endings shown here are possible conclusions for the samples shown on the previous Worksheet.

1. Summary—use a few words to remind the reader what the essay has covered: *Packing for a vacation doesn't have to be a difficult chore. Follow these simple suggestions and you will no longer dread coming face-to-face with those empty suitcases.*

2. Signal the end with a question or a striking statement: *These are the main groups in most middle schools. Which one do you belong to, and is this where you'll be stuck for the rest of your life?*

3. Certain words or phrases, such as *in conclusion, as you can see, it is clear, therefore,* signal an ending: *As you can see, no one should have to eat the sort of food that is served in our cafeteria. With a few changes, our kids can get meals that make them healthier and happier.*

PART TWO—TRY IT YOURSELF: On the previous Worksheet, you wrote beginnings for three essays. Choose the same three topics and write an ending for each. Use one of each kind of ending shown in the samples above. Circle your three choices below:

How to Lose a Friend
The Best TV Shows of the Season
The Toughest Characters on TV
My Favorite Games
The Best Kinds of Pets
What Kind of Allowances Should Kids Get?
A Day at the Mall

ENDING 1:_____

_____

_____

_____

ENDING 2:_____

_____

_____

_____

ENDING 3:_____

_____

_____

_____

ASK THE EXPERT

PART ONE: What do you know a lot about? Is there some subject you know more about than most people your age? What are your hobbies? What do you like to do after school? Is there some subject you have read about—pets, sports, movies, whatever? Perhaps you like to read mysteries or sport stories or science fiction. Do you help out at home, cooking or fixing things? Do you know how to take a bike apart and put it together again? Do you play a musical instrument? What do you do in the summer? Do you know all the rules of some sport or game? Have you ever gone camping? Do you know how to put up a tent or build a fire? Are there any arts or crafts you can do? In the box below, write down any subjects or activities you think you know fairly well.

PART TWO—BRAINSTORMING: Choose one of the subjects above. Circle it. Prepare a brainstorming list for it below. Include items about how you first became interested in this subject or activity and what you like about it. Show your completed list to the teacher before writing the essay.

_____

_____

_____

_____

_____

_____

_____

_____

_____

_____

_____

PART THREE—FIRST DRAFT: When you write your essay, remember that most people will not know as much about this subject as you. Include all the information they need in order to understand. Write about this subject using as much detail as possible. Use a separate sheet of paper.

MAKING CHANGES

PART ONE: Nobody's life is perfect. There are probably lots of things in your life that you'd like to change if you could. Start by writing down some of the things you'd like to see changed around home:

_____

_____

_____

_____

Next, list some of the things you'd like to see changed around school (such as homework, bell schedule, lunchroom, etc.):

_____

_____

_____

_____

_____

PART TWO: You're going to write an essay that expresses how you feel about one or more of these things. If you write it convincingly, maybe you'll be able to persuade someone to make the changes you want. First, decide which "gripe" you're going to write about. Circle it above. Then prepare a brainstorming list for this essay. Include all the reasons you can think of why this change is needed, and how it can be brought about:

_____

_____

_____

_____

_____

_____

Which items on your brainstorming list are most important? Which are less? Put numbers next to the items on your list, making the most important 1, 2, and so forth.

PART THREE: On a separate sheet of paper, write the first draft of an essay about the change you'd like to make. Be sure to give details of why and how these changes should be made. Try to be convincing!

MAKING BIGGER CHANGES

DIRECTIONS: For the previous assignment, you wrote an essay about some changes you'd like to see made in your home or school. Now, you're going to begin to think about bigger changes. What would you like to see changed about your town? Are there problems your community needs to solve? Maybe your town needs a playground or a town pool or more convenient shopping. Then, look beyond your own community. What about this nation, even the whole world? Do you think our planet is perfect? What should be changed? On the lines below, write down some of the things you would like to see changed in your community, country, or world.

_____

_____

_____

_____

_____

_____

_____

Now, draw a circle around the item that you feel most strongly about. Prepare a brainstorming list below for an essay about this idea.

_____

_____

_____

_____

_____

_____

_____

Number the items on the brainstorming list in the order of importance. Using a separate sheet of paper, write the first draft of an essay about the change you would like to see in your community, nation, or world. Present your most important ideas first. Try to be as convincing as you can. Maybe you will persuade others to think as you do.

WHAT DO YOU THINK?

DIRECTIONS: Choose one of the statements below, and circle it. Then, write an essay telling whether you agree or disagree with this statement. Try your best to convince your reader that your opinion is the correct one. Give as many reasons as you can to back up your stand. Support your argument with examples.

Boys are better than girls in every way.

Homework is a waste of time.

It's better to have one good friend than be part of a group.

_____

_____

_____

_____

_____

_____

_____

_____

_____

_____

_____

_____

_____

_____

_____

_____

_____

_____

Name_____ Date_____

WHAT DO YOU THINK?

DIRECTIONS: Choose one of the statements below, and circle it. Then, write an essay telling whether you agree or disagree with this statement. Try your best to convince the reader that your opinion is the correct one. Give as many reasons as you can to back up your stand. Support your argument with examples.

The U.S. will have a woman as president soon.

Teachers are usually fair.

Children should not watch TV on school nights.

_____

_____

_____

_____

_____

_____

_____

_____

_____

_____

_____

_____

_____

_____

_____

_____

_____

_____

_____

_____

_____

_____

_____

EXPANDING AN IDEA

DIRECTIONS: Several topics are listed below. Next to each topic is a brainstorming list.

TOPIC	*BRAINSTORMING LIST*
HOME	happy, family, parents, house, apartment, rooms, roof, windows, kitchen, furniture outside, porch, street, lawn, garage, trees, children, private arguments, pets, meals, bedroom, chair, table, bed, together, alone
HEALTH	important, food, exercise, medicine, doctor, body, heart, lungs, stomach, vitamins, diet, energy, hospital, junk food, old age, milk, cereal, fruit, fish, meat, chicken, eggs, breakfast, lunch, dinner, pure, fresh air, positive attitude, illness, disease
SPORTS	team, fun, friends, school, playground, ball, racquet, bat, swimming, baseball, season, football, injury, hiking, tennis, golf, pitcher, ball field, Little League, bicycling, watching or playing, competition, muscles, excitement, practice, skiing, ice skating, Olympics, basketball, sneakers, clothes, prize fighting, soccer, track and field, racing, wrestling, sports movies, sports TV, gymnastics, stars

Choose one of the topics above for an essay. Circle the topic you have chosen. Then, follow the directions below.

1. What part of this topic will my essay concentrate on? (Examples: For HOME, you might focus on a description of your house, or how the members of your family get along. For HEALTH, you could concentrate on good health habits, or on healthy eating or on getting sick, etc.) Write your focus here:_____

    _____

    _____

    _____

2. Circle the words in the brainstorming list above that you will be using in your essay. Add any more ideas that you might use. (You can write these in the margins.)

3. Now you are going to expand this idea into an essay. Write your first draft on a separate sheet of paper. Can you put down your thoughts in a clear and detailed manner? When you have completed your first draft, your teacher will assign you to a critiquing group where you can get suggestions for revising.

Name_____   Date_____

EXPANDING AN IDEA

DIRECTIONS: Several topics are listed below. Next to each topic is a brainstorming list.

TOPIC	*BRAINSTORMING LIST*
TELEVISION	screen, controls, channels, entertainment, cartoons, sitcoms, news, favorite programs, announcer, actors, actresses, commercials, sports, weather, movies, VCR, violence, cops, families, kids, sci-fi, aliens, homework, music, groups, singers, rock, video games
FRIEND	pal, buddy, need, boy, girl, fun, important, groups, best friend, understanding, laugh, like, love, get along, depend on, support, confide, games, sports, free time, visit, school, home, help, hang out, sharing, talk, popular group, companionship, help
SUMMER	warm, hot, sunny, vacation, camp, sports, games, friends, family, pool, lake, shore, hike, travel, read, sleep, play, happy, boring, bike, baseball, daydream, hobbies, trips, car, train, plane, boat, canoe, row, relax, nap, holiday, firecrackers, flag, Independence Day, fireworks, picnics, park

Choose one of the topics above for an essay. Circle the topic you have chosen. Then, follow the directions below.

1. What part of this topic will my essay concentrate on? (Examples: for TELEVISION, you might focus on what you like best about television, or how kids are affected by TV; for SUMMER, you might concentrate on what you enjoy doing in the summer, or summer sports, etc.) Write your focus below:

_____

_____

_____

_____

2. Circle the words in the brainstorming list above that you will be using in your essay. Add any more ideas that you might use. (You can write these in the margins.)

3. Now you are going to expand this idea into an essay. Write your first draft on a separate sheet of paper. Can you put down your thoughts in a clear and detailed manner? When you have completed your first draft, your teacher will assign you to a critiquing group where you can get suggestions for revising.

4

PREPARING A WRITER'S NOTEBOOK

Almost all professional writers keep notebooks, journals, or workbooks. These are the repositories of journal-type entries, and can also be used to jot down thoughts, ideas, interesting words, felicitous phrases, snatches of conversation, etc. before they are forgotten. Robert Louis Stevenson said, "All through my boyhood and youth...I kept always two books in my pocket, one to read, one to write in....Thus, I lived with words. And what I thus wrote was for no ulterior use, it was written consciously for practice."

Journals and notebooks are invaluable to the student as source books for their writing. Most students have become familiar with diary-type journal writing, but a journal is only one type of notebook. The notebook that will be prepared and developed in this chapter will be used as a collection of lists, references, writing aids, and records that student writers will be able to draw on again and again to nourish and enlarge their writing skills. This notebook should outlive the particular course for which it is being prepared. It can be a student's companion, reference work, and writing aid for years. Those students for whom writing holds an important place in their lives may find this notebook to be the first of many. Even students with no special interest in writing will discover that the work they do in this notebook will give them a better feeling about words and possibly a new sense of written expression as something that can be fun and exciting.

It is imperative that you instill a positive attitude about these notebooks before beginning the compilation. Be enthusiastic. Tell the students they will have fun with these books. Encourage them to choose a notebook that appeals to them aesthetically. Your students might want a notebook that is red or black or has a picture of their favorite rock group on the cover. It can be a looseleaf binder, or one that is bound. Tell them to choose something that appeals to them, even if they don't know why. Suggest that this will release innate writing skills they may not even know they possess. Who knows? You might be telling them the truth. Once the notebook has been established and framed out, it lends itself to many exercises and lessons, and can be used to reinforce curriculum work.

The first activity, setting up the writer's notebook, should be completed before any of the other projects are attempted. Once the skeleton of the notebook has been prepared, the various sections may then be attacked in any order. Since most of the notebook sections are open-ended, you can bring them into play whenever the need arises to bring certain types of writing practice into line with a curriculum or to reinforce specific writing skills.

Above all, encourage the students to develop a sense of this notebook as a personal and ongoing vehicle for their individual thoughts, feelings, and jottings, and as a handy reference book for all their writings. The writer's notebook should *not* be subject to grading. Here the student can feel free to learn through trial and error, to make mistakes, to use less polished writing as a bridge to acquiring fluency. By all means, make comments and suggestions for improvement, but nothing will stifle the natural creative process more than composing for a grade rather than writing for better self-expression. If you feel that students need some sort of grade as a prod to getting their work done, you might wish to assign a pass or fail grade only, based on a minimum required amount of work in the notebook.

Activity 1   SETTING IT UP

The first activity consists of setting up the skeleton of the notebook and getting it ready for use. This should be completed before any of the other notebook activities are attempted. The Worksheet is, to a great extent, self-explanatory. Most seventh- and eighth-graders should be able to do this either as a class project or at home. Younger students will probably need to be guided through this activity. The students may be curious as to how the various sections are going to be used. Don't get bogged down in explanations at this point. Tell the students that their questions about each heading will be answered when they actually begin to work on that section.

PREWRITING ACTIVITIES

1. Inform the students about this activity several days in advance so they will have time to get a notebook. Encourage them to select a notebook that appeals to them, as described above. It is important to be enthusiastic so that the students will believe that they are beginning something that is special, important, and perhaps permanent. If you are working with groups that tend to be forgetful, it might be wise to send a notice home with the students. Be sure that all students have their books ready before beginning.

2. Distribute Worksheet 4-1 SETTING IT UP. Fourth-, fifth-, and sixth-graders should work as a group on this activity, as you lead them through each of the notebook headings. For seventh- and eighth-graders, you have the option of following the same procedure or of permitting them to follow the Worksheet directions on their own. If you follow the latter course, check each notebook for accuracy before beginning any subsequent activities.

3. Younger students may wish to do some illustrations, particularly on the title page, if time permits. They will enjoy this, and it will help to personalize the notebook for them.

Activity 2   STRONG, ACTIVE VERBS

Good writers avoid the passive voice. The verb *to be* is one of the dullest, most uninteresting words in the English language. Sometimes you can't avoid its use, but students should be discouraged from using it and other passive verbs whenever more active, more exciting ones are available. *There is a girl* is weak compared to *A girl lounges, A girl runs, A girl strolls*. Can *There is a flower* compare to *A flower droops, A flower blooms,* or *A flower opens*?

In this activity, students will compile a list of active verbs in their notebooks. This list can be expanded whenever students come across new, interesting verbs. It can also be used for reference whenever they are writing, but even if they do not consult it in the future (since most of us are too lazy to do so except out of desperation), just the act of compiling this list will make students more aware of the effective use of verbs in their future writings.

PREWRITING ACTIVITIES

1. Write the following sentence on the chalkboard:

   Jack sees the book.

2. Ask the students to substitute a word or phrase for *sees* that would make the action more specific. Write the suggestions on the chalkboard. These may include *notices, stares at, peers at, eyes, studies, glances at,* etc.

3. Instruct students to open their notebooks to the section headed "Active Verbs."

4. Distribute Worksheet 4-2 ACTIVE VERBS. Read the directions aloud. Instruct the students to transfer the words on the Worksheet into their notebooks as directed, to add additional active verbs, and to construct at least three original sentences for each group of verbs. Remind the students to leave room for additional words at the end of each list.

Activity 3   BEAUTIFUL WORDS/UGLY WORDS ——————————

A meager vocabulary is limiting to a writer. Of course, young students are at an early point in their acquisition of language. It is never too soon, however, to acquire the feeling for words that makes the expansion of one's vocabulary desirable and exciting. People who enjoy writing usually love words. They derive pleasure from the sound and the shape of words. Some of them even like spelling drills! Like Wordsworth, they are entranced by "choice words and measured phrase."

Most children, of course, do not have such a passionate devotion to language. Too often, that which could be sweet and thrilling becomes dull and unpleasant. Children need to experience words as fun. This notebook section makes a game out of vocabulary building, and students never fail to plunge into it with ready acceptance and enthusiasm.

PREWRITING ACTIVITIES

1. Describe to the students how words can mean different things to different people. Give examples, such as the word *anaconda*, which may sound lovely to someone who is fascinated by snakes, but slimy and horrible to someone who hates reptiles. *Asparagus* may have a sweet connotation to one who loves the taste of this green vegetable, while it may actually disgust a person whose taste buds are revolted by it. Emphasize that it is not merely the meaning of a word, but even the way it sounds that could make the word appealing to one person and unpleasant to another. Give several examples of words that you find personally agreeable, and others that seem unattractive. I usually like to use *serendipity* and *loquacious* as examples of words that fall on my ears with delight. *Igloo, bludgeon,* and *grubby* seem harsh and grating to me. (This often leads to great curiosity about the meaning of these words, and some quick vocabulary enhancement right then and there.)

2. Write headings for two columns on the chalkboard, as follows:
   Beautiful Words   *Ugly Words*
   Elicit from the students words that they believe fit into each of these categories. It is not necessary for the students to defend or give reasons for their choices. The same word may appear in both columns as the result of a difference of opinion among two students. Develop at least five words in each category. This will not be difficult. Students usually rush into this activity with enthusiasm.

3. Have the students turn to the section of their notebooks labeled "Beautiful Words/Ugly Words." Instruct them to begin their own personal list of words they like and dislike. (They may borrow words from the chalkboard, if they wish.) They should amass a minimum of seven to ten words in each column by the end of this lesson. Some of the students may want to use dictionaries, which is fine and should be encouraged.

4. Most groups will want to share their words. Students are usually eager to read their own lists aloud and to hear the lists of others.

5. Try to sharpen the students' awareness of the sound of words by encouraging them to keep this list open-ended and to add to it whenever they come across a word that fits into either category.

You may wish to do this as a class activity occasionally when there are five or ten extra minutes available.

Activity 4   SENSORY WORDS

We are all sensory beings. Our five senses—touch, sight, taste, hearing, and smell—are the doors through which we perceive the world. They are also the tools that a good writer uses to gain entry into the reader's world, opening the mind and heart of the reader to what the writer wishes to communicate. Turn to any page in any well-written book and you are sure to find a judicious use of sensory language. Becoming comfortable and familiar with a variety of sensory words will enable the student to turn out prose and poetry that is vivid and immediate to the reader.

PREWRITING ACTIVITIES

1. Elicit from the students the names of the five senses and write them on the chalkboard.
2. Write the following sentences on the chalkboard:
   She switched off the stereo; the music died with a scratchy moan.

   Sarita's brain was a confused blob of mush.

   A small, thin girl with tangled hair and pale, teary eyes shuffled over.

   Nick had long, blonde hair that curled softly behind his ears.

   The toy wooden boat bobbed on the gentle ripples.

   The sour, pungent smoke filled the room, stinging her eyes.
3. Ask the students to pick out the sensory words in these sentences and identify which sense is involved. Underline or circle these words on the chalkboard. Discuss how some words can apply to more than one sense (e.g., *blob, scratchy*).
4. Instruct the students to open their notebooks to the section labeled "Sensory Words."
5. Distribute Worksheet 4-4 SENSORY WORDS. Read the directions aloud.
6. This activity is rather long and cannot usually be completed in one session. To sustain student interest, work on one or two senses at a time. After each session, the students will enjoy sharing their sentences.

Activity 5   SIMILES

Any word that appears to have literary or intellectual connotations is sure to fall unpleasantly on the ears of an average group of students. What typical child wants to appear literary or intellectual? The mere mention of a topic such as "similes" is enough to bring forth groans of despair. Yet, the ordinary conversation of average people is peppered with similes—"as hungry as a wolf," "as quiet as a mouse," "as cold as ice."

The everyday nature of similes creates an additional problem for the writing teacher who is trying to help students develop creativity. Many similes have been used so much that they have become worn out. The examples above are representative of overused, boring similes. When beginning to use similes, students' first attempts will probably be similarly trite. Most of them will immediately offer *blood* as a simile for *red*, or *grass* for *green*. This is acceptable as part of the learning process, but from the outset, encourage greater originality. The writer's notebook is a useful tool for practice and experimentation with figures of speech such as similes and metaphors. It is a nonthreatening environment, one that, with gentle stimulation from the teacher, can encourage creative experimentation. Later, the students can turn to the collection of similes they have compiled in their notebooks and use those that are appropriate to whatever writing project may be at hand.

"Oft on the dappled turf at ease," wrote William Wordsworth, "I sit and play with similes." We dont' expect our students to become literary giants. With the help of the notebook, however, perhaps they, like the poet, will come to take pleasure in "playing" with similes.

PREWRITING ACTIVITIES

1. Write the word *similes* on the chalkboard. Ask students for a definition and examples.

2. Distribute Worksheet 4-5A SIMILES. Read the directions for Part One (underlining similes). When completed, have students share results.

3. Read the directions for Part Two. Discuss the excitement and challenge of unusual similes versus those which have been overused.

4. Share completed similes.

5. Distribute Worksheet 4-5B MORE SIMILES. Read and discuss the directions.

6. Share completed paragraphs. Suggest that students continue to add to their lists whenever they think of or come across interesting similes. Encourage students to use these lists as a reference for writing assignments.

Activity 6   METAPHORS ─────────────────────────

"All slang is metaphor, and all metaphor is poetry." One doesn't have to agree with Chesterton's assessment of the poetic values of slang to recognize the prolific use of metaphor in daily language. "A bee in her bonnet," "his bark is worse than his bite," "striking out on a job interview," "hold your horses,"—the list of metaphors we use as a matter of course could go on and on.

Metaphors can enrich writing and make it more exciting and interesting to both the reader and the writer. If presented to students as an ordinary, commonly used figure of speech rather than a literary device, the use of metaphor can add creativity and enjoyment to student writing.

PREWRITING ACTIVITIES

1. Write the following sentences on the chalkboard:
   Get lost!
   That kid's a real devil.
   I was late to school, so I flew all the way.
   That fighter is a tough cookie.

2. Explain that a metaphor is a comparison that calls one thing by the name of another. Point out that in the preceding sentences, no one is literally going to become lost, the child is not really Satan, the speaker does not sprout wings, and no one is going to eat the fighter. Thus, these are metaphors. Sometimes, it helps to write next to each example another sentence where the same word is *not* used as a metaphor, such as:

He was lost in the woods.
The Satanist said that the devil made him do it.
The bird flew into the tree.
My mom baked chocolate cookies.

3. Distribute Worksheet 4-6A METAPHORS. Read the directions for each section aloud. As each part is completed, share the results.

4. Distribute Worksheet 4-6B MORE METAPHORS. Read and discuss the directions. When completed, have students share the results.

5. Encourage students to record in their notebooks any new metaphors they think of or come across in their reading or conversation. Suggest the use of this section of their notebook as reference material for writing projects.

Activity 7   DESCRIPTIONS

NOTE: Activities 4, 5, and 6, involving sensory words, similes, and metaphors, should be successfully completed before commencing descriptions. The vocabulary enrichment and skills acquired in these previous activities will aid the students greatly when attempting to write descriptions.

Descriptions are grist for the writer's mill. Attempts to convey one's impressions of landscapes, objects, and people, either real or imaginative, lend themselves to all sorts of colorful word combinations. The writer's notebook is a perfect vehicle for this activity. It is a place where the student-writer can feel free to try out various combinations of words and phrases and find those that best express his or her inner vision.

Most of us have difficulty taking a scene that is vivid in our minds and transferring it to paper in words that will convey our own exact impressions to the reader. The key is practice. One learns to write by writing…and writing…and writing. Combined with the growing awareness and skills of self-evaluation that are fostered by the process method, this constant practice inevitably leads to improved communication skills.

PREWRITING ACTIVITIES

1. Read aloud an evocative description of place. You may choose one with which you are familiar, or read the following (from the author's book, *Catch A Dancing Star*):

   The main studio at Madame Sophie's School of Ballet was a room of mirrors. Three entire walls were composed of nothing but mirrors—giant pools of reflection reaching all across and top to bottom. In the mirrors could be seen other mirrors reflecting the first mirror in an endless tunnel of silver images.

2. Ask the students to discuss what makes this description vivid. Ask for specific words and phrases that help to create an atmosphere, a feeling for the place. (It may be necessary to read the paragraph a second time.) Ask them to identify any sensory words, similes, or metaphors. Write these on the chalkboard.

3. Follow the same procedure for a description involving a person or a group of people. Choose an excerpt with which you are familiar, or use the following marvelous description from *A Tale Of Two Cities*. (After all, what writer can compare with Dickens when it comes to describing people?)

He was a man of about sixty, handsomely dressed, haughty in manner, and with a face like a fine mask, a face of transparent paleness; every feature in it clearly defined; one set expression on it. The nose, beautifully formed, otherwise, was very slightly pinched at the top of each nostril. In those two compressions, or dents, the only little change that the face ever showed, resided. They persisted in changing color sometimes, and they would be occasionally dilated...; then, they gave a look of treachery and cruelty to the whole countenance.

4. Distribute Worksheet 4-7 DESCRIPTIONS. Read aloud the Worksheet directions for Part One. Stress the importance of using a wealth of details and vivid language to create a tapestry of rich images. (Be sure that the students answer the questions and follow the directions that follow the list of suggested topics.)

5. When Part One has been completed, allow those students who wish to do so to share their descriptions with the others.

6. Read aloud and discuss the Worksheet directions for Parts Two and Three. Follow the same procedures as for Part One. Don't expect the polished, final-draft-type writing one hopes to find in hand-in assignments. The students should, at all times, feel that the notebook belongs to them, not you. They should be encouraged to experiment, to take chances, to try out their writing wings.

7. Encourage students to write additional descriptions in the notebook whenever time permits or when some scene is vivid in their memories. This could be a suggested activity when there are a few free moments during subsequent class periods.

Activity 8   DIALOGUE

Watch youngsters in a library. When faced with a choice of which book to read, most of them will unhesitatingly choose one with lots of dialogue. Dialogue is easy to read. It seems to make the pages turn faster. It gives the reader a sense of intimacy, of being a part of the action. It moves the story along and gives insight into the characters in a fairly painless way. (Also, as any veteran of book report assignments knows, dialogue takes up more room.)

Young people also like to include dialogue in their own original stories. It *seems* to them like an easy, natural way to show how characters are acting in any particular scene. Notice the emphasis on the word *seems*. The young writer's enjoyment in creating a scene sustained mostly by conversation is rarely matched by success in execution. In such scenes, the reader too often has no idea who is saying what, where these characters are, and what they are doing.

Writing dialogue is definitely not as simple as it appears. Even adult writers who may have facility in narrative writing often fail to produce effective dialogue. A few simple rules and suggestions, however, can help anyone, at any age, to develop better skills in using this technique. In the "Dialogue" section of the writer's notebook, students will have an opportunity to improve their ability to write dialogue through practice and experimentation.

PREWRITING ACTIVITIES

(For Worksheet 4-8A DIALOGUE: WHO'S SAYING WHAT?)

1. Ask which students enjoy seeing dialogue in the books they read, and like to use it in the stories that they write. There will assuredly be a large show of hands. Tell them that they are going to use their writer's notebooks to learn how to write better and clearer dialogue.

2. Distribute Worksheet 4-8A DIALOGUE: WHO'S SAYING WHAT? Read Dialogue One aloud. Ask the students to suggest what is wrong with this dialogue as it is written. Elicit the fact that it is not always clear who is speaking.

3. Ask the students to edit Dialogue One right on the Worksheet, penciling in information in the appropriate places that will clear up the confusion. Read and compare results.

4. Do the same with Dialogue Two.

5. Read aloud Worksheet directions for dialogue-writing practice in the writer's notebook.

6. When all the students have completed one dialogue scene, divide the class into critiquing groups of three or four students each. Have the participants read their dialogues aloud while the others in the group evaluate whether they have succeeded in making clear at all times who is speaking.

PREWRITING ACTIVITIES

(For Worksheet 8B DIALOGUE: PLACE AND ACTION)

The neophyte writer usually has a vague sense of where the scene is taking place, what activities are occurring, and how the characters are behaving, but fails to write any of it down, believing perhaps that the reader will somehow acquire this knowledge through osmosis or ESP. Usually, the beginning writer doesn't know that there is anything wrong with the scene, and doesn't realize that the details that are in the writer's mind are not being made clear to the reader. This needs to be pointed out, time and time again.

As with any other facet of writing, practice is all-important for writing effective dialogue. Students also need guidance and direction. The purpose of this notebook activity is to help students acquire skill in transmitting through dialogue a sense of place, time, movement, and character.

1. Distribute Worksheet 4-8B DIALOGUE: PLACE AND ACTION

2. Read aloud the first dialogue. Elicit from the students the facts as to what action is taking place in this scene, where it is occurring, and what sort of activities the characters are engaging in.

3. Read the second dialogue on the Worksheet aloud. Ask the same questions as listed above, and elicit from the students the fact that the excerpt does not provide this information.

4. Ask the students to edit the second dialogue right on the Worksheet, inserting whatever words, phrases, and sentences they feel are needed to add a sense of action, place, and character.

5. Share and discuss the edited versions.

6. Read and discuss directions for writing an original dialogue in the students' notebooks.

7. When completed, share the original dialogue scenes. Discuss how a sense of action, place, and character has or has not been achieved in each example.

Activity 9   SCRAPBOOK

How often does it happen that we read an interesting passage or see a stimulating photo and determine that this is something we will always remember, only to forget it under the pressures of time and a multitude of other stimuli? "Listen to this!" I'll sometimes exclaim, and read aloud an excerpt that is so wonderful that it must be shared. Two days later, however, when I try to recall this unforgettable prose, it will have disappeared from my consciousness unless I find some way to preserve it.

In this activity, students will learn a way to preserve for future reference those jewels of writing that would otherwise be lost forever.

SCRAPBOOK PREPARATION ACTIVITIES

1. Prepare or read to the class a few interesting quotes or passages that you have clipped from newspapers or magazines. Explain that you cut these out because you liked them a lot, and wanted to keep them on file for future reference or when you might wish to refresh your memory about their content.

2. Ask the students how many of them have ever read something they wished they could remember, but later forgot. Have the students turn to the scrapbook section of their notebook. Tell them that this section is there to help them preserve things they have read, heard, or seen that they might want to use someday in their own writing.

3. For this activity, have available in the classroom a supply of old newspapers and magazines, and, of course, scissors and paste. Set the students to work clipping and pasting into their notebooks any phrases, sentences, paragraphs, photos, and illustrations that they find stimulating and/or memorable. You can also make available, though not for cutting, books, pamphlets, song sheets, and the like from which students might wish to copy passages or lines.

4. Suggest that the students use this section of their notebooks whenever they come across something they would like to preserve that might be helpful in their own writing.

SETTING IT UP

Follow the directions below for setting up your notebook.

Title Page. Center, on the first page:

WRITER'S NOTEBOOK
AND
BOOK OF LISTS
OF
_____
(your name)

Number the remaining pages 1–39 and write the following headings on the pages indicated:

Page 1. STRONG, ACTIVE VERBS
Page 4. BEAUTIFUL WORDS/UGLY WORDS
      (Set up two columns as shown below, left.)

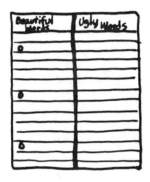 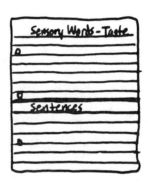

Page 5. SENSORY WORDS—TASTE (Draw a line half-way down the page and write
      "Sentences," as shown above, right.)
Page 6. SENSORY WORDS—TOUCH (same arrangement)
Page 7. SENSORY WORDS—SMELL (same arrangement)
Page 8. SENSORY WORDS—SOUND (same arrangement)
Page 9. SENSORY WORDS—SIGHT (same arrangement)
Page 10. SIMILES
Page 12. METAPHORS
Page 14. DESCRIPTIONS
Page 20. DIALOGUE
Page 24. SCRAPBOOK

Name_____ Date_____

ACTIVE VERBS

DIRECTIONS:

1. Each of the passive verbs below is followed by a list of active verbs with which it can be replaced. Copy these lists into your notebook.

2. Can you think of other active verbs that would be better than these passive ones? Write these additions at the end of each list.

3. Leave several lines blank after each list. (You can use this space to keep adding active verbs as they occur to you.) Then, write *at least three sentences* using some of the active verbs on your list.

SEE: stare, glance, observe, notice, examine, glimpse, gaze, peer, peek, squint, watch, inspect, recognize, study (Can you think of other active "see" verbs? Write them here):

_____

_____

GO: walk, run, stroll, skip, hop, budge, flit, slide, glide, travel, roam, ramble, march, plod, tramp, toddle, drive (Add more active "go" verbs here):

_____

_____

BE: exist, live, breathe, sit, stand, relax, strive, work, stay, inhabit, visit, perch (Add other active "be" verbs here): _____

_____

HAVE: hold, gain, win, collect, find, pick, take, inherit, steal, grab, clutch, grasp, grip, hoard, pile up, gather, catch, seize (Can you think of other active "have" verbs? Write them here):

_____

_____

EAT: swallow, devour, chew, gulp, pick at, chew, nibble, graze, crunch, bite, gnaw (Add any other active "eat" verbs you can think of):

_____

_____

SPEAK: shout, murmur, whisper, yell, bark, declare, lecture, recite, croak, rasp, order, sing, breathe, pronounce, cry, scream (Add other active "speak" verbs here): _____

_____

Whenever you hear a new, interesting active verb, or come across one in your reading, try to remember it, and add it to the list in your notebook.

SENSORY WORDS

DIRECTIONS:

1. Copy the lists of sensory words from this Worksheet into your notebook on the appropriate page. (Write all *touch* words on the upper half of the notebook page labeled "Sensory Words—Touch"; write all *smell* words on the upper half of the page labeled "Sensory Words—Smell," etc.)

2. Can you think of sensory words that are not on this Worksheet? Add them to the lists in your notebook.

3. On the lower portion of each page, under "Sentences," write at least *five* sentences. Each sentence should contain at least one sensory word from the list. Can you think of sentences that use more than one sensory word?

SENSORY WORDS—TASTE: peppery, salty, sweet, sour, biting, spicy, vinegary, minty, fruity, nutty, grainy, smooth, flavorful, pungent

SENSORY WORDS—TOUCH: cold, icy, hot, warm, smooth, rough, nubby, grainy, sandy, moist, dry, satiny, silky, tickly, velvety, slippery, oily, uneven, jagged, prickly, hairy, shaggy

SENSORY WORDS—SMELL: mouth-watering, musky, smoky, sharp, sweet, greasy, musty, pungent, rotted, fragrant, vinegary, woodsy, spicy

SENSORY WORDS—SOUND: ring, toll, blare, blast, clang, chime, whisper, sizzle, scream, screech, yell, tinkle, crash, hiss, hum, roar, bellow, shout, whine, moan, uproar, boom, siren, thunder, ear-splitting, rustle, babble, purr, clap

SENSORY WORDS—SIGHT: flaming, golden, bloody, rosy, shadows, sunny, moonlit, hazy, grainy, light, dark, dim, bright, starry, glowing, flash, flicker, silhouette, glare, glow, blaze, shimmer, dazzle, radiance, murky, gloomy, cloudy, foggy, and all colors—red, blue, green, yellow, etc.

SIMILES

PART ONE: A simile is a direct comparison, usually using the words *like, as,* or *than.* Copy the following sentences into your notebook on the page headed "Similes" and underline the similes.

1. Her cheeks were as rosy as a desert sunrise.

2. The room was furnished elegantly, like a French castle.

3. He was as happy as a toddler with a new toy.

4. The Man of Steel moves faster than a speeding bullet.

PART TWO: Make up your own original similes by copying and completing the following phrases in your notebook. Try to think of exciting, original phrases. For example, "as big as a hero's heart" is better than "as big as a giant," and "cold, like a January morning in the mountains" is more interesting than the ordinary "cold, like ice." Make your similes as fresh and creative as you can.

as disgusting as _____

as creative as _____

swift, like _____

as messy as _____

uglier than _____

as exciting as _____

as embarrassed as _____

wrinkly, like _____

angrier than _____

as unusual as _____

as friendly as_____

as cruel as_____

beautiful, like_____

as successful as_____

MORE SIMILES

DIRECTIONS: Copy the following paragraphs into your notebook, changing the words printed in italics into similes. (For example, *awesome* might become *as awesome as the entrance to a castle*.)

1. Mark hesitated before knocking. The huge, carved door was *awesome*. Mark wondered if he had any right to be here. He tried to straighten out his creased jacket. He realized that it was *shabby*. Mark was *poor*. From the looks of this mansion, Freddy was *rich*. Mark took a deep breath. He took hold of the big, brass knocker and rapped it *loudly* against the wood.

2. Mimi loved her grandmother's kitchen. It was *big* and *old-fashioned*. Pots of all sizes hung from the ceiling. The fruits on the counter looked *tasty*, and the smells coming from the oven were *heavenly*.

3. Pat and Zach were tossing baskets. The playground was *crowded*. Three older guys came over. They looked *tough*. The biggest one said, "Move over, kids." His voice was *loud* and *mean*.

4. Eddie sat in the back of the classroom. The movie was *boring*. He was glad the room was *dark*. Nobody noticed that he wasn't watching. He was looking at the girl who sat at the end of the row. There was something about her that was *strange*.

5. Mike was *tired*. They had been hiking for hours, and his legs felt *heavy*. The pack on his back was *big*. "Are we stopping soon?" he inquired. The counselor glared at him. His eyes were *hard*. "Not yet," he said *angrily*.

6. Andrea waited her turn at bat. She was *nervous*. She hadn't had a hit all day, and this game was *important*. Now, in the ninth inning, her team was losing. Things looked *bad*. Then, the girl before her hit a single. The crowd was *wild*. Andrea stepped up to the plate. She held her bat *tightly*, and waited for the pitch.

7. The police officer was *tall*. His expression was *grim*. He grabbed Bobby's wrist *tightly*. "Come with me, kid," he growled. Bobby was *terrified*. He tried to pull away *desperately*. The cop's grasp was *firm*. "I didn't do anything," Bobby moaned.

METAPHORS

PART ONE: Copy the following sentences into your notebook under the heading "Metaphors." Underline the metaphors.

1. The sergeant barked commands to his men.

2. The farmer disliked the roar of city streets.

3. My mother is an angel.

4. The student sailed through the test.

PART TWO: The following lines are from poems by well-known authors. Each poem contains one or more metaphors. Can you find them all? Copy these excerpts from poems into your notebook, and underline the metaphors.

> I think that I shall never see
> A poem lovely as a tree.
> A tree whose hungry mouth is prest
> Against the earth's sweet-flowing breast...
> —Joyce Kilmer

> I heard the trailing garments of the Night
>   Sweep through her marble halls!
> —Henry W. Longfellow

> See the mountains kiss high Heaven
>   And all the waves clasp one another...
> —Percy Bysshe Shelley

> Fresh from the dewy hill, the merry year
> Smiles on my head, and mounts his flaming car...
> —William Blake

PART THREE: In your notebook, write at least five original sentences that contain metaphors. You may choose from the suggestions below, or come up with your own ideas.

• A sentence describing how your father looked when he found out you had lost his favorite book

• A sentence describing an exciting moment in a baseball (or football) game

• A sentence describing a teacher facing an unruly class

• A sentence describing your best friend's face

• A sentence telling how you felt when you found out you had failed a test

MORE METAPHORS

PART ONE: Underline the metaphors in the following sentences.

Sergeant Preston was a big, shaggy bear of a man.
Tim was an Eagle Scout and a real straight arrow.
A blanket of heavy mist lay over the island.
It was a tough day; I felt ready to fall apart.
That dress is a knockout.
That poor guy is up the creek without a paddle.
Don't get carried away by that happy thought.
The street was an oven on that ninety-degree day.
They slithered across the dance floor to the music.

PART TWO: In your notebook, write at least five original sentences that contain metaphors. You may choose from the suggestions below, or come up with your own ideas.

• A sentence describing a haunted house.

• A sentence describing something you saw on the way to school today.

• A sentence telling about a fight you had with a friend

• A sentence describing how you feel about chores you have to do at home

• A sentence describing the taste of some medicine

• A sentence describing how your house looked after your last birthday party

• A sentence telling about a scary dream you had

• A sentence describing how kids feel on the last day of school

• A sentence describing a shopping mall

• A sentence describing your room at home

DESCRIPTIONS

PART ONE: Turn to the section of your notebook headed "Descriptions." You are going to write a description of a place you know well. It could be a real place, or it could exist only in your imagination. Before you begin writing, close your eyes for a moment and try to visualize this place in your mind. Notice every detail, no matter how small. Include all these details in your description. You may choose one of the following places, or any other place you wish:

Your room at home
One of your classrooms
A park you have recently visited
A house you wish you could live in
A place that frightened you
A place where you felt safe and happy
A winter landscape
A summer landscape
The street you live on
The town in which you live
A ballpark

When you have finished writing your description, answer the questions below as honestly as you can. If your answer to any of them is "no," return to the description in your notebook and make any changes needed.

1. Would someone who has never seen this place be able to visualize it clearly from my description?

2. Have I used any sensory words (touch, taste, smell, sound, sight) in my description?

3. Have I used vivid adjectives?

4. Have I used any similes or metaphors?

PART TWO: In your next description, be sure to use *at least* two sensory words, one simile, and one metaphor. You may again describe any place (real or imaginary) that you know well, or you may choose another of the subjects listed above. Try to make your description vivid by using colors and shapes. Tell how this place makes you feel.

PART THREE: Your next description will not be of a place, but a *person*. Try to make your description so vivid that a reader will be able to see this person as clearly as you do. You may describe a real person, one you have dreamed about, or one who exists in your imagination. Don't limit yourself to this person's physical appearance. Describe his or her personality, interests, and activities. How do you feel about this person? How does he or she treat you? Use vivid adjectives, sensory words, and at least one simile or metaphor in your description.

DIALOGUE: WHO'S SAYING WHAT?

When using dialogue in a story, it is important that the reader be aware of who is speaking. In the two dialogues below, this is not always clear. You are going to fix this by inserting words or phrases, or even sentences, wherever you think they are needed to identify the speaker. Do this right on the Worksheet with a pen or pencil.

DIALOGUE ONE

Alex tore out of the house, slamming the door behind him. A few seconds later, Pat came running after him.

"Why did you take off like that?" There was no answer. "Where are you going?"

"I don't know."

"I'm coming with you."

"Do whatever you want."

"I wish you'd talk to me."

For a while, they walked side by side in silence.

"Why won't you tell me what happened?"

"Forget it."

"I wish I could forget it, but I can't." His upper lip twitched nervously.

"Neither can I."

DIALOGUE TWO

The park was beautiful. The lilacs and cherry blossoms were all in bloom. Bonnie and Amy walked along the petal-strewn path.

"Smell those lilacs."

She took a deep breath. "M-m-m. They're heavenly. I'd like to pick a few and take them home."

"Don't do that!" she said sharply. "It's a public park."

"So, who'd know?" She smiled slyly, reached up, and pulled off a deep-purple lilac.

She looked around nervously. "Now you did it. We're going to get into trouble."

She shook her head. "What a stick you are! You're just no fun at all."

NOTEBOOK PRACTICE: Turn to the dialogue section of your notebook. Write a dialogue scene between two or more people. Name the characters at the beginning. Use your own idea, or choose one of those suggested below:

1. Two kids spot a ten-dollar bill in the street and grab it at the same time. Each claims that it is his.

2. A brother and sister, alone in the house, hear an intruder come in.

3. Two friends who haven't seen each other for over a year meet at a party.

DIALOGUE: PLACE AND ACTION

Read the following dialogue scene. Be prepared to discuss how the writer achieves a sense of time, action, place, and character. Underline the words, phrases, or sentences that do this.

"It's a bad sprain. I'm afraid you're going to be hobbling around for a few weeks," said the doctor, as he taped Ellen's foot and ankle.

"A few weeks! But I must be able to dance by next week!" cried Ellen.

The doctor shook his head. "Impossible," he told Ellen in a gentle but firm tone that left no room at all for doubt.

"Oh, Mom!" Ellen cried after the doctor had left. "What will I do? Next Monday is the day that Madame Sophie announces her decision. I'm supposed to dance for her and Mr. Bolard."

Mrs. Stone hugged her daughter sympathetically. "I'm sorry, dear, but there's nothing to be done. You'll just have to accept that."

But Ellen was inconsolable. "It's all my fault!" she wailed. "I did it to myself. I was just plain careless!" She turned away.

In the next dialogue, the writer fails to give the same sense of action, time, place, and character. Read it, and then be prepared to discuss why it does not succeed.

Mike saw Andy. "Hi," he said.

"Hi," Andy replied.

"Are you ready?"

"Yeah. Are you?"

"Okay, Let's get started."

Andy was all set. So was Mike.

NOTEBOOK ASSIGNMENT: Turn to the next dialogue page in your notebook. Write a dialogue where you show time, place, and action. Show where the conversation is taking place and what the characters are doing while they are talking. You may choose a scene of your own, or use one of the following:

- A conversation between a strict teacher and a student who has not handed in an assignment on time.

- A conversation between three friends who are planning a party.

- A conversation between a coach and some of the team members just before an important game.

5
JOURNAL
WRITING

Journal writing has been called a way of talking to oneself, an individual dialogue that offers a concrete expression of thoughts, impressions, feelings, and ideas. Journal writing is also a way to relive experiences. Confronting these experiences a second time on paper not only helps one to understand them, but is also a path to more skillful writing, since one writes most easily about what one knows best.

Many students confuse a journal with a diary. Diary writing can be one aspect of a journal, but the journal is much more than that. It is not merely a log where one jots down the date followed by a list of activities: *I got an A on the math test this morning. In the afternoon, I went to Becky's house. Angela was there, too. We played Monopoly. Then I went home. We had roast beef for dinner.* In a journal, these things would be examined. How did the writer feel about getting that A? What did the teacher say about it? What is Becky like? What is Angela like? Are they all best friends? Why or why not? Who won the game? How did the writer feel about that?

The guided activities in this chapter will encourage students to use the journal in a way that will benefit them more in terms of self-understanding and development of writing skills.

Activity 1 EARLIEST MEMORIES

Ray Bradbury, the popular science-fiction writer, has claimed that he can remember back to the day and moment of his birth. Most of us do not have that sort of total recall, but we do have memories of our early years. These memories can be joyful or sad, exhilarating or terrifying. Sometimes they are buried under years of repression and blocking. With practice, such as that provided by journal writing, these experiences can be unearthed and examined. Almost always, these explorations help writers to a better understanding of who and what they are. Such understanding promotes clear thinking and clear, inspired writing.

Adults sometimes find this activity threatening at first; youngsters almost always plunge into it with verve.

PREWRITING ACTIVITIES

1. Have the students bring in blank notebooks, or supply them with small composition books to use as journals. Tell them that many well-known writers developed their writing skills, at least partially, through journal writing. Discuss the confidential nature of this notebook, and assure them that while you may check these pages for amount of writing, you will never read the content, unless specifically requested by the student. You will probably want to inform the students, however, that this confidentiality does have certain legal limits. For example, if you read something that suggests a student is being abused or neglected, you have a legal obligation to report it.

2. Distribute Worksheet 5-1 EARLIEST MEMORIES. Read aloud the directions for Part One—Stimulating the Memory.

3. When Part One has been completed, some students will wish to share their responses. (Younger students, in grades four, five, and six, will probably be more open about this. Seventh- and eighth-graders have more of a sense of privacy.) Provide a time for sharing with those classes and students that want it. Do not, under any circumstances, put pressure on students to participate. Emphasize that the exercise was primarily to help them remember past events.

4. Read and discuss directions for Part Two—Notebook Activity. Encourage the use of as much detail as possible about people, clothing, background, dialogue, etc. as students can recall.

5. Some students may wish to share their memories with the class. Again, younger children are often eager to do so, and time can be allotted to reading aloud when the activity has been completed. The older students will probably want to keep their journals inviolate, and this feeling should be respected.

Activity 2   RECENT MEMORIES

The previous project stimulated students to recall their earliest memories. This activity will get them started writing about more recent events in their lives. In many ways, this is a much easier activity since the details are so much fresher in their minds. They will not have to devote so much energy to digging for a memory, and will, therefore, have more time to give shape and form to what they write.

This Worksheet will be particularly useful for students who seem to be blocked when faced with a blank page in a journal. They'll tell you they have nothing to write about. This is, of course, nonsense. Everyone's life, young or old, is filled with a myriad of experiences and events. These youngsters are just not accustomed to making the transition from memory to written word. This activity should guide them through and beyond that hurdle.

PREWRITING ACTIVITIES

1. Ask the students if any of them have been unconscious for the past week. Of course, in every class there will be at least one child who will raise his or her hand. But the point will have been made.

2. Tell the students that since they have been alive and awake for the past week, they have seen and done many things during that time period. Now, they are going to write about them.

3. Distribute Worksheet 5-2 RECENT MEMORIES. Read the directions for Part One together. Tell students that this exercise will help them remember some of these experiences.

4. When Part One of the Worksheet has been completed, some time can be allotted to the sharing of answers. Fourth-, fifth-, and sixth-graders will probably want to do so. Older students may not, and any person's wish for privacy should be respected.

5. Read and discuss the directions for Part Two of the Worksheet. Encourage the use of details and emotional responses. Interrupt several times during the writing period to ask, "How did this make you feel?" This will stimulate the students to include more material about their feelings.

6. After this assignment has been completed, encourage the students to continue to record recent events on their own time. In addition, whenever there are five or ten minutes left over in a class period, this activity can be continued.

Activity 3   THOUGHTS AND FEELINGS ———————————————

The previous activity (Recent Memories) was designed to help students make a habit of writing in their journals. It encouraged them to record recent happenings in their lives. This is easy to do since these events are still fresh in the students' minds. Ultimately, however, we don't want the students to use their journals for mere shopping lists of events. If your students can be persuaded to dip into the reservoir of their own inner selves, they will be writing about things that are meaningful and important to them. People of all ages become better writers when the subject they write about is deeply felt.

PREWRITING ACTIVITIES

1. Write on the chalkboard:

   in the doctor's waiting room:
   taking a math test:
   planning a surprise party:
   coming up to bat:
   playing video games:

2. Ask the students to remember the last time they went to the doctor. Ask them for words that describe their feelings while sitting in the waiting room. Write these words on the chalkboard next to *in the doctor's waiting room*. Ask for a few similes that describe their feelings, such as "helpless, like someone who is tied up." Write these on the chalkboard.

3. Follow the same procedure with the next four phrases (*taking a math test, planning a surprise party, coming up to bat*, and *playing video games*).

4. Ask the students to suggest other situations. Add these to the list and follow the same procedures.

5. Distribute Worksheet 5-3A THOUGHTS AND FEELINGS. Read and discuss the directions for Part One.

6. When Part One has been completed, suggest some sharing, especially with younger students. Do not pressure the students to do so, as this could inhibit the free flow of thoughts, ideas, and feelings. The students *must* feel comfortable and secure in their privacy to get the most from journal writing.

7. Read and discuss the directions for Part Two of the Worksheet.

8. Distribute Worksheet 5-3B MORE THOUGHTS AND FEELINGS. Read and discuss directions for Part One.

9. When Part One has been completed, share results if desired. Then read and discuss the directions for Part Two.

Activity 4   I'LL NEVER FORGET ———————————————

Some students need little or no direction with journal writing. The instruction, "Open your notebook to the journal section and write about anything you wish," is enough to send their pens scratching over the paper like madly scampering hens' feet.

Other students, however, meet such a suggestion with blank looks and equally blank pages. They need direction and examples. They require specific activities that will help them break through reluctance and inertia, and aid in the recall of events to record in their journals.

PREWRITING ACTIVITIES

1. Inform the students that you are going to tell them about an event in your life that you have never forgotten. Then, choose an incident that will hold their attention and relate it, using descriptive details about the place and people involved. Choose a situation to which the students can relate. An evening at the symphony or the day your divorce was granted would not really be of tremendous interest to middle- and junior-high-school-age boys and girls. I sometimes relate a humiliating incident in the third grade when I was mistakenly accused of some misbehavior, was hauled down to the principal's office, and my parents were called in. I enliven the narrative by revealing how shocking and unfair this seemed to the "goody-goody" child I was. Or, I tell about my anger on the night my dog woke us all up with loud barking, and how my husband threatened to get rid of the dog, only to discover in the morning that ours was the only house on the block that had not been burglarized. By being open with students about emotion-arousing events in your own past, you will make it easier for them to find and reveal similar incidents in their own lives.

2. Read aloud the following excerpt from *The Diary of a Young Girl* by Anne Frank. It is an honest description of feelings with which most youngsters can identify.

   I am the subject of nearly every discussion.... Nothing about me is right; my general appearance, my character, my manners are discussed from A to Z....Am I really so bad-mannered, conceited, head-strong, pushing, stupid, lazy, etc., etc., as they all say? Oh, of course not... If you only knew how I sometimes boil under so many gibes and jeers. And I don't know how long I shall be able to stifle my rage. I shall just blow up one day.

3. Discuss the above, and encourage students who wish to do so to talk about incidents in their own lives that made them feel strong emotions, such as anger, fear, joy, etc.

4. Distribute Worksheet 5-4 I'LL NEVER FORGET. Read aloud and discuss the directions for Part One of this Worksheet.

5. When they have completed Part One of the Worksheet, some students, particularly the younger ones, may wish to share their work. Permit them to do so, if desired.

6. Read and discuss the directions for Part Two. Emphasize the effectiveness of details to help students sharpen their memories of the event.

Activity 5 DREAMS AND NIGHTMARES

Dreams are intensely personal things. What better place is there for recording them than the pages of a journal? Dreams are fun to write about because they are not bound by the limits of real, waking life. The images are often bizarre, disconnected, and surrealistic, like a painting by Dali. They can stimulate the imagination and usually lend themselves to the use of evocative words and interesting phrases.

Some students may be resistant to this activity at first. They may claim that they never dream or, more likely, that they don't remember any of their dreams. The prewriting and Worksheet activities in this section are designed to break through this reluctance. Once started, almost everyone finds that they enjoy writing about their dreams. The more they get into it, the more fun it seems to become.

PREWRITING ACTIVITIES

1. (Optional) The day before, tell the students that they are going to write about their dreams. Suggest the following techniques for remembering dreams:

    a. Just before going to sleep, visualize in your mind a dream you would like to have. You may not experience this particular dream, but experts say that doing this will help you remember what you did dream when you awaken.

    b. Put note paper and a pen near your bed. When you awaken, *immediately* write down your dream. The longer you wait before writing, the less you remember.

2. Read aloud the following excerpt from *Kubla Khan* by Samuel Taylor Coleridge:

   In Xanadu, did Kubla Khan
   A stately pleasure-dome decree:
   Where Alph, the sacred river ran
   Through caverns measureless to man
      Down to a sunless sea.
   So twice five miles of fertile ground
   With walls and towers were girdled round:
   And there were gardens bright with sinuous rills,
   Where blossomed many an incense-bearing tree;
   And here were forests ancient as the hills,
   Enfolding sunny spots of greenery.

Tell the students that in this poem Coleridge recorded the images he had seen in a dream. Ask the students to talk about any beautiful scenes they have seen in dreams. Some of them may wish to relate horrible or frightening scenes they remember from dreams.

Tell the students that many people believe that dreams are significant and can help us gain better self-understanding, *if we can remember them*! The best way to recall dreams is to write them down.

3. Distribute Worksheet 5-5 DREAMS AND NIGHTMARES. Read aloud and discuss the directions for Part One.

4. When Part One has been completed, some students (especially the younger ones) may wish to share some of their answers. Do not pressure any students to do so.

5. Read and discuss the directions for Part Two. Encourage the students to describe their images in as much detail as possible.

Activity 6   TELLING THEM OFF ─────────────────

Everyone has fantasies of "telling them off." After the fact, we think of the clever things we could have said to the rude clerk in the supermarket.

Children are no different from adults when it comes to unexpressed feelings and opinions. In fact, their needs in this regard are often greater. Children are usually in the inferior position. They must show respect to their elders (although it seems that old-fashioned virtue might be on the way out). A child who "tells off" a teacher or a parent is considered "fresh" or "sassy." That may very well be the case, since the child's judgment is immature. Nevertheless, the emotions are real, and so is the young person's need to express them.

A journal can be a vent for these feelings. It can give the writer a chance to write down those dialogues that are forbidden in real life. It is important that the writer feel safe. Johnny is not going to be able to tell Mr. Grump, the teacher who yelled at him a couple of hours ago, what he thinks of him if he has even the slightest fear that Mr. Grump will see his literary outburst. The students should be assured that what they record will be read by no one but themselves.

PREWRITING ACTIVITIES

1. Ask the students how many of them have ever wished they could "tell off" someone who has treated them unfairly or been mean or rude to them. (Many hands will wave immediately.) Discuss why it is not always possible to tell people exactly what we think of them and/or their actions. Ask the students how it makes them feel to have to hold back their strong feelings.

2. Read aloud the following excerpt from Anne Frank's *Diary Of A Young Girl*:

   I'm boiling with rage, and yet I mustn't show it. I'd like to stamp my feet, scream, give Mummy a good shaking, cry, and I don't know what else, because of the horrible words, mocking looks, and accusations which are leveled at me repeatedly every day....I would like to shout, 'Leave me in peace...!' But I can't do that, they mustn't know my despair, I can't let them see the wounds which they have caused, I couldn't bear their sympathy and their kindhearted jokes, it would only make me want to scream all the more.

Discuss the writer's feelings and how she was helped by recording these things in the journal.

3. Tell the students that today they will have the opportunity, in the privacy of their journals, to vent feelings and opinions that they may have to hold back in real life. Distribute Worksheet 5-6 TELLING THEM OFF. Read and discuss directions for Part One—Warming Up. Tell them that this Worksheet is for their use only and does not have to be turned in. Discourage the students from asking others to show them their answers, as some children may feel pressured to do so, if asked.

4. When Part One has been completed, read and discuss the directions for Part Two. Assure the students that their writings here are private and confidential and will not be read by anyone else.

Activity 7   WISHING ON A STAR

The dreams that appear at night are not the only ones that offer fertile ground for writing. Those that come during the day are equally fascinating. We all daydream from time to time. Even adults have moments where they succumb to fantasies of what might be.

For children, rigid boundaries have not yet been erected around the possibilities of their lives. They daydream a lot more than adults. Their imaginations are often fired by the books they read and the films and TV they see. It's easy to picture oneself as Indiana Jones, charging on horseback through a horde of evil Nazis. It's fun to imagine oneself, a world-famous actor, making an acceptance speech for an Academy Award. Children love to "wander in that golden maze," as the poet Dryden called the act of daydreaming.

PREWRITING ACTIVITIES

1. Ask the students how many of them ever find themselves daydreaming about people, places, or events other than where they are at the moment. Many hands will immediately shoot up. Assure them that everyone, even teachers, sometimes engage in this pleasurable activity.

2. Ask the students where they would wish to be if they could be anywhere else at this moment. Tell them to close their eyes briefly and try to picture that place in their minds. Then, encourage some of the students to describe that place and their reasons for wishing to be there.

3. Tell the students that no matter how hard they may wish to be elsewhere, there is no way that they can be anyplace else right now but the classroom they are in. (Be prepared for groans at this point.) Suggest that some wishes, however, can come true. Initiate a discussion about ways in which this might happen. They will probably come up with "luck," "hard work," etc. Suggest that there is nothing wrong with daydreaming (in the appropriate place and time), and that many later achievements and careers began as youthful daydreams.

4. Read aloud the following quotation from Henry David Thoreau:

If you have built castles in the air, your work need not be lost; that is where they should be. Now put the foundations under them.

Discuss the writer's meaning. Ask if any of the students have ever had wishes or daydreams that later came true, and how this happened. If you feel comfortable doing so, relate something appropriate from your own experience.

5. Instruct the students to close their eyes again. This time, ask them to picture themselves as they would wish to be a month from now, or a year from now, or ten years from now. Encourage students to share and discuss some of their ideas with the others, if they wish to do so.

6. Distribute Worksheet 5-7 WISHING ON A STAR. Read and discuss the directions for Part One.

7. When Part One has been completed, some students may want to share their responses.

8. Read the directions for Part Two. Encourage students to expand on their wishes with many details.

Name_____ Date_____

EARLIEST MEMORIES

PART ONE—STIMULATING THE MEMORY: Everything that has ever happened to you becomes part of who you are, what you know, and how you feel. The more you can remember about your past experiences, the more comfortable the present will feel. Some people claim to remember things that happened to them when they were tiny infants. Most of us can't recall that far, but there are events and people from long ago that stay in the memories of even the most forgetful of us.

You can use your journal to live your life over again. Once you start practicing and bringing forth memories, you will find yourself remembering more and more. The activities on this Worksheet will help you recall experiences you thought you had forgotten.

Complete the following by filling in the blanks. Try to be as honest as you can. (You will not have to show this Worksheet to anyone.) Try to fill in all the blanks, even if you are not sure that your answer is accurate.

1. I remember a toy I had when I was very young. It was a _____. I think its color was

   _____. I must have been about _____ years old.

2. I remember a person who scared me when I was very young. He (She) was _____.

   Whenever I saw this person, I was afraid that _____.

3. The earliest memory I have of my mother is _____.

4. The earliest memory I have of my father is _____.

   _____.

5. The earliest memory I have of a brother or sister or friend is _____.

6. I remember feeling happy when _____

   _____. I must have been about _____ years old.

7. I remember going to _____ when I was about _____ years old. It was _____.

PART TWO—NOTEBOOK ACTIVITY: Think back to the earliest experience you can recall. It can be one of those above, or something else. It may help to close your eyes for a few moments and try to clear your mind. When you are ready, begin writing down this experience in your journal. Use as much detail as you can remember about where it was happening, who was there and how they looked, and how you felt. Probably, as you write, you will remember more and more. Write it down. Your writing doesn't have to follow any rules or form. This is for your eyes only.

_____

_____

RECENT MEMORIES

PART ONE: Everyone has many experiences each day. Some of these events may be important. ("On Monday, I fell off my bike and broke my right arm.") Other things may not seem important at all. ("This morning I had Cheerios for breakfast. Mom and Dad ate English muffins. I told them I'd be home late because I had band practice after school.") But they all happened. A journal gives you the opportunity to relive these occurrences. When you experience an event a second time, in your journal, you may discover that it was more important than it seemed the first time around. This exercise will help open your mind to reliving all the times of your life. Complete the thoughts below by filling in the blanks. Write something in every space. Be honest. Only you need see this.

1. On my way to school this morning, I saw a _____, a _____, and a _____.

2. Last night, my mom (or dad or guardian) _____.

3. On Sunday, I _____.

4. The best thing that happened this week was when _____.

5. The worst thing that happened this week was when _____.

6. Here are three things I have done in the last hour:

   I _____;

   I _____;

   and I _____.

PART TWO: Now that you have begun to think about recent events in your life, it's time to start recording them in your journal. On the first empty page in your journal, describe one or more things that happened during the past week. You can use some of the ideas above or others.

Try to recall and write down as many details as you can—who was there, what people were wearing, how they looked, what sounds you heard, where you were, and what objects you could see. If you can't think of anything to write about, just write down everything that has happened since you awoke this morning.

Record everything, no matter how dull it seems. Use lots of detail, and describe your feelings. The more you write, the more you will begin to remember, and the more important it will all become.

_____

_____

_____

_____

_____

Name_____ Date_____

THOUGHTS AND FEELINGS

PART ONE—REMEMBERING

DIRECTIONS: For each of the descriptions below, try to remember the last time you were in that situation. Think about how you felt and what you thought. In the space below description 1, write down all the words and phrases (not complete sentences) you can think of that describe your thoughts and feelings at that time. Then, do the same for each of the other situations.

1. being in a room with people I don't like

```
[                                                                    ]
```

2. being blamed for something I didn't do

```
[                                                                    ]
```

3. watching my favorite TV program

```
[                                                                    ]
```

4. waking up the first morning of a vacation

```
[                                                                    ]
```

5. meeting a new friend

```
[                                                                    ]
```

PART TWO—PUTTING IT IN THE JOURNAL

DIRECTIONS:

1. Choose one of the situations in Part One. Write about it in your journal. Tell exactly what happened and how you felt. Try to remember all the thoughts and feelings you had at the time. Make yourself relive that time by describing your thoughts and feelings in as much detail as possible.

2. Do the same with as many of the other situations in Part One as you have time for. Choose those you remember best.

MORE THOUGHTS AND FEELINGS

PART ONE—REMEMBERING

DIRECTIONS: Look at the descriptions below. Try to remember the last time you were in each of these situations. Recall the way you thought and felt at the time. In the space below each situation, write as many words and phrases as you can that describe your thoughts and feelings.

    1. taking a trip with my family

    2. being in a place that made me feel good

    3. being in a place that made me feel sad

    4. giving a wrong answer in class

    5. getting into a fight or argument

PART TWO—PUTTING IT INTO THE JOURNAL

DIRECTIONS

    1. Choose one of the situations in Part One. Write about it in your journal. Tell exactly what happened and how you felt. Try to remember all your thoughts and feelings at the time. Help yourself to relive that time by describing your thoughts and feelings in as much detail as you can. Try to use some similes, if possible.

    2. Do the same for as many of the other situations as you can. Write about your strongest impressions first.

I'LL NEVER FORGET

PART ONE—GETTING IN TOUCH: When something happens that makes you have strong feelings, you probably remember that event for a long time—perhaps forever! This activity will help you recall some of these times, even if you think you've forgotten them.

All you have to do is fill in the blanks in the sentences below. You'll be surprised at how much you'll begin to remember.

1. I'll never forget the first time I _____

_____

2. I remember how angry I was when my father _____

_____

3. No one knew that I cried when _____

_____

4. I was so surprised when my friend _____

_____

5. Once, when I was alone in my house, I_____

_____

6. I was so ashamed when _____

_____

7. I was really scared when _____

_____

8. My happiest day of the past year was when _____

_____

9. I'll never tell anyone about the time _____

_____

PART TWO: Choose one of the events in the list above and write about it in your journal. Use lots of details as to where it happened, who was there, how they looked, what was said, how you felt, etc. The more details you use, the more you will remember.

DREAMS AND NIGHTMARES

PART ONE: *Everybody* dreams. Some people remember their dreams better than others. We all remember some dreams or parts of dreams that really made an impression. How much do you remember about your dreams? This exercise will help you recall some interesting dreams.

Fill in the blanks below. If you cannot remember an answer, make one up. Just pretending may help you remember a real dream.

1. I was once frightened by a _____ in a dream.

2. The strangest place I ever saw in a dream was _____.

3. Once, I dreamed that my mom _____

_____

4. The worst dream I ever had was one where _____

_____

5. I felt sad after I dreamed that _____

_____

6. Last night, I think that I dreamed about _____

_____

7. I saw a man in a dream who looked like _____

_____

8. I love dreaming about _____

_____

9. I hate dreaming about _____

_____

10. I saw an animal in a dream that looked like _____. I felt _____

when it _____.

PART TWO: In your journal, describe any dream you can remember. You'll find that the more you write, the more details you will recall. You can write about more than one dream if you wish. Try to describe the images that come into your mind, even if they seem strange.

Name_____   Date_____

TELLING THEM OFF

PART ONE—WARMING UP: Haven't you sometimes wished that you could tell people what you really think of them or of something that they have done? You can't always do that because it might be disrespectful or hurt their feelings or get you into trouble. You can do it in your journal, however, without hurting anyone. No one but you will ever see what you have written, but getting it off your chest could make you feel a lot better. The exercise below will help you organize your thoughts and decide exactly who you would like to "tell off" in your journal. Just fill in the blanks.

1. I wish I could tell my dad that he _____

_____

2. I wish I could tell my mom that she _____

_____

3. If I could tell _____ what I really thought of him (her), I'd say that _____

_____

4. I get really annoyed with my friend, _____, when _____

5. Sometimes, _____ acts like such a _____

_____

6. I feel angry when _____ treats me like _____

_____

7. _____ doesn't know how ridiculous it is when _____

_____

8. One person I really can't stand is _____ because _____

_____

PART TWO: Choose one of the people or situations above (or any other that you feel strongly about). In your journal write a pretend conversation where you say what you really think and feel. You are safe because you are the only one who will ever see this (unless you yourself want to show it to somebody).

WISHING ON A STAR

PART ONE: Can wishing make it so? Nobody knows for sure. Yet, everyone daydreams at times, whether it does any good or not. It's wonderful to imagine ourselves smarter, stronger, and more attractive than we are at the moment. It's fun to picture the wonderful or exciting things we wish we could do. Your journal is a perfect place to record your wishes and daydreams. Just writing down these wishes in detail can make them seem more likely to happen. Part One of this Worksheet will exercise your mind and help you remember some of the daydreams you may have had. Just fill in the blanks. If you cannot think of an answer, make one up. Even a made-up answer can sometimes help to bring back forgotten daydreams.

1. I wish I could be more like _____

   because _____

2. Sometimes, I like to imagine that I am in _____. I feel _____ to be there

   because _____

   _____

3. Sometimes, I like to pretend that I am a _____ and I picture myself _____

   _____

4. If I could be a _____, I would be _____ and here's what I would do. I would

   _____

5. One place I like to picture in my mind is _____.

   It is _____ and _____. I like it because _____

   _____

6. My deepest wish is that _____

   _____

PART TWO: Use your journal to record one or more of the daydreams above (or any other that you may wish to recall). Try to write down as many details as you can. Describe the place you are in, yourself and the others who are there, and what happens. Record any conversations you imagine, and tell how these daydreams make you feel.

6

JOURNALISM

Journalism refers to the gathering of news, writing articles, and editing and publishing a newspaper or other periodical. It also includes writing feature articles, editorials, interviews, sports, and book, TV, and film reviews.

The study of journalism involves learning the specialized rules that apply to this type of writing. In some respects, these differ from the laws of composition as taught in English classes. Students who are accustomed to the structure of the formal essay with its introductory and closing paragraphs and topic sentences may, at first, be confused by the pyramid form of a news article and the nature of leads. Good writing is good writing, however, and journalistic writing with its emphasis on combining factual accuracy, pertinent detail, clarity, and high-interest stylization is a worthwhile experience for the student-writer.

Journalism is a highly effective tool for motivating children to write because they usually love it. They have no trouble at all picturing themselves as Lois Lane churning out the news at the *Daily Planet*, or as part of a growing company of well-known TV journalists whose faces have become as familiar and comforting as members of the family.

The activities in this section are not, of course, meant to constitute a complete course in journalism. They offer supplemental materials that can be effectively utilized with any journalism curriculum, they can stand on their own as a brief excursion into journalistic territories, or they can be the backbone for preparing a class or group to produce a class or school newspaper.

Any teacher who has attempted to develop a curriculum or teach journalism at grades below high school level knows that while there are many fine journalism texts for high school and college classes, there is a dearth of material available for elementary, middle, or junior high schools. The author developed most of the materials in this chapter during fourteen years of serving as advisor to a middle school newspaper and teaching journalism to eighth-graders. These projects have all been tested over and over again in the laboratory of the real classroom. Through the years, they have been modified and altered until what remains (what you are presented with here) are those that have proven most motivational and effective.

At the end of this chapter, you will find some comments and advice for producing a school newspaper.

Activity 1   PLUNGING INTO THE NEWS

This activity can serve to introduce the students to the idea of journalistic writing. No previous training or experience is required. There will be no requirements to meet any journalistic standards in the presentation. The purpose of these Worksheets is motivational. The students will have fun doing them, and will, hopefully, develop a positive attitude toward this kind of writing.

PREWRITING ACTIVITIES

1. Tell the students that they are all going to become reporters.

2. Distribute whichever of the following Worksheets seems most appropriate for the class. Worksheets 6-1A and 6-1B usually work best for grades four, five, and six. Seventh- and eighth-graders should have no trouble with Worksheets 6-1C and 6-1D.

3. Read and discuss the directions at the top of each Worksheet. These are simple and self-explanatory. Most groups should be able to tackle these Worksheets on their own.

4. Permit those students who wish to do so to share their work with the class. Discuss which stories the class likes best, and elicit why these seem to work better than others. Usually, the better stories will have more action and detail, and a clearer structure and organization.

5. This activity is meant to stimulate interest in journalism. Do not, therefore, go through any of the steps of the process writing method here. No critiquing or revising is necessary. Look on this activity as a warm-up drill.

6. If desired, distribute the second Worksheet for the particular age group of your class, and go through the same procedure. Some seventh- and eighth-grade classes may enjoy doing the Worksheets meant for the younger children, and vice versa.

Activity 2   LEADS ─────────────────────────────

Beginnings are often said to be the most crucial part of any piece of writing, whether fiction or nonfiction, short story or full-length novel. The beginning will determine whether the reader will go any further. If readers become bored or confused, they will stop reading (except, of course, for teachers, who have to plow through everything to the bitter end, no matter how mind-numbing it may be).

This is even more true for newspaper writing. Someone who has invested money or time in a book may force himself or herself to continue, for a while anyway, in the hope that things will pick up as the pages are turned. This is not the way newspapers are read. Average newspaper readers do so on the run, and have no intention of reading everything on the page. Their eyes dart about until they fasten on something that quickens their interest. The beginning of a newspaper article (called a *lead*) must, therefore, be compelling enough to grab the readers' attention and make them want to read on. If the first few sentences discourage readers, they will jump to another item, no matter how good the rest of the story may be. The lead must also express the essential core of the news story. In a sense, the lead is the story itself, in a nutshell. It is a summing up which is done not at the end but at the beginning, and it must be written in such a way as to have an impact on the reader.

There are several different types of leads that are commonly used. It would be helpful if, prior to this activity, newspaper articles were brought into class and various leads read and discussed. Students will be motivated and inspired by studying real articles from real newspapers with which they are familiar. You may even want them to copy a good news article, as this may direct their attention to the structure. However, this is not essential. The Worksheets in this activity will offer examples of each kind of lead, and will guide the students in writing their own leads.

PREWRITING ACTIVITIES

1. Distribute Worksheet 6-2A SUMMARY AND QUESTION LEADS.

2. Read and discuss Part One—Definition and Essential Elements. Emphasize the dual function

of a lead to provide the core facts in a skeletal form, and to do so in an exciting, stimulating way. Write on the chalkboard the key words: *Who? When? What? Where?*

3. Read Part Two—Types of Leads. Discuss how each example on the Worksheet goes about grabbing the interest of the reader and how it answers the questions Who? What? When? Where? Write on the chalkboard the responses to these questions as contained in each lead.

4. Read and discuss the directions for Part Three. Be certain the students understand that in this exercise, they are going to be writing *only leads*, not complete stories.

5. When the leads have been completed, read a selection of them to the class (with or without identifying the writer according to your own discretion), and discuss whether they succeed in catching the reader's interest and in telling Who? When? What? Where? You can use small peer critiquing groups for subsequent lead exercises. Since this is the first activity, however, it will be helpful to discuss the results with the whole class to be certain that the students get some insight into what makes a good lead. Follow this with regular process method revising steps as previously described.

6. Follow the same procedure with Worksheets 6-2B QUOTATION AND PICTURE LEADS, 6-2C SHOCKING AND HUMOROUS LEADS, 6-2D LIVELY LEADS, and 6-2E YOUR BEST LEADS, except that these results can be shared in small critiquing groups.

Activity 3   THE NEWS STORY

The basic techniques of good writing are the same, no matter what the genre. News writing, however, has some specific rules of its own.

A news article aims to capture the attention of average readers and hold their interest as long as possible. Sentences are short and to the point. Paragraphs are brief. Wordiness is a no-no. This may appear simple at first glance. However, much must be done with little. Words have to be chosen with special care for their impact on the reader.

A lead must be attention-grabbing and, at the same time, summarize the most important facts. The remainder of the article is written in the "inverted pyramid" form, with the most important details first and the least important at the end. At all times, the utmost emphasis must be on accuracy, brevity, and the truth.

Students may be confused at first by the special needs of news writing. Contraction, rather than expansion, must be mastered. Objectivity is essential. The latter concept is often difficult for young students. They are constantly inserting their own judgments or the word *I* into their news writing. It takes practice on the part of the students and vigilance on the part of the teacher for these students to learn that in a news story the reporter usually presents the facts of the story without reference to his or her own person or ideas. The procedures and Worksheets in this activity will lead the student toward that goal.

PREWRITING ACTIVITIES

1. Write the words *News Article* on the chalkboard. Below it, draw an inverted pyramid:

2. At the top of the pyramid, write *Lead*. Review the purpose and form of the lead.

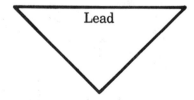

3. Tell the students that in a news article, the facts are related in order of their importance. The most important facts are found in the first paragraph, the least important at the end. Illustrate this on the chalkboard by filling in the pyramid as follows:

Most important fact first;
second most important
fact next; and so
on down to the
least im-
portant
fact

4. Discuss the reasons for this arrangement. Try to elicit these from the students, but conclude with two basic reasons, the first being the limits of newspaper space and the fact that an editor can chop off from the bottom of an article, if necessary, knowing that only the least important facts will be cut. The second reason is from the point of view of the readers. Those who have only time and interest for the main facts can get these by reading the first portion of the article; readers with greater interest in the details can read the entire piece.

5 Write on the chalkboard:

Short Sentences
Short Paragraphs
Eliminate Unnecessary Words

6. Write the following pairs of sentences on the chalkboard. For each, discuss why the second sentence is more readable and effective than the first:

The FBI agent accompanied the group of witnesses to Scranton last month because the FBI was hopeful that it might work out that some of them might be able to identify the suspects in the crime.

The FBI agent accompanied the witness to Scranton last month, hoping they could identify the suspect.

When the play was over, everyone in the audience seemed to be happy and showed by enthusiastic clapping that they had enjoyed the performance.

At the end of the play, the audience clapped enthusiastically.

7. Write the following on the chalkboard:

Who?
What?
Where?
When?
(Why?)
(How?)

Review the first four *W*'s, which the students have already used in their leads. Tell them that many journalists believe there should be a fifth *W* (*Why?*) and an *H* (*How?*). Tell the students that in their news writing, they must always use the first four *W*'s. The last two items are desirable, but may sometimes be omitted.

8. Write on the chalkboard the words *I* and *Me*. Tell the students that these words never appear in a news story unless they are part of a quote from one of the people involved in the story. They must never refer to the writer. Tell them that the story must be about the people and events involved, and almost never includes the reporter. Say that this also includes the writer's opinion. Write the following groups of phrases on the chalkboard:

She had beautiful blonde hair and blue eyes.
She had blonde hair and blue eyes.

The mean man allegedly beat his children.
The man allegedly beat his children.

Mr. Smith convincingly states his innocence.
Mr. Smith states his innocence.

Discuss how the first sentence in each group includes the writer's person or opinion, and how this can be avoided as it is in the second sentence of each group.

9. Distribute Worksheet 6-3A THE NEWS STORY. When the students have completed both parts of the Worksheet, correct and discuss their answers to the questions in Part Two.

10. Distribute Worksheet 6-3B ANALYSIS OF NEWS ARTICLE. (You will need to have newspaper articles available for this activity. You can make copies of a news story so that the students will all be analyzing the same one, or you can distribute different clippings among the class, or you can have the students bring in their own articles or do this as a homework assignment.) Reading and analyzing a professionally written article in this way will set the stage for student writing.

11. Distribute Worksheet 6-3C WRITING A NEWS STORY. Read and discuss Part One.

12. Read and discuss the directions for Part Two.

13. When the students have completed their news stories, divide into critiquing groups and follow the process writing steps for revising and rewriting.

14. Distribute Worksheet 6-3D WRITE ANOTHER NEWS STORY. Follow procedures as outlined in steps 11 to 13.

Activity 4   FEATURE STORIES

The feature story differs from a news article in ways that make it appealing to young and mature reporters alike. The rules are looser and there is more leeway for creative, personal style and structure. A writer's sense of humor, wonder, or amazement can be transferred to the reader in a feature article. In many ways, features resemble the type of essay writing to which students are accustomed and feel comfortable.

On the other hand, since more time and creativity can be brought to bear on a feature, there are greater expectations. Feature writing has to be more polished and more carefully worded than news reporting. Also, it generally requires more research and more interviewing than a regular news story.

PREWRITING ACTIVITIES

1. Write the following headlines on the chalkboard:

   EPA Rules Ocean City Beaches Unsafe for Entire Summer
   A Resort Town Responds to a Season Without Tourists

Discuss the differences in focus between stories based on each of these headlines. Elicit the fact that the first story tells about a specific news event (the ruling) and must report this news as soon as it happens. The second story can be written any time during the summer and can go into much detail about the effect of this ruling on the town and its people. Explain that this is called a feature story.

2. Distribute Worksheet 6-4A GUIDELINES FOR FEATURE WRITING. Read and discuss Part One—How to Write a Feature Story.

3. Read the directions for Part Two. When the students have completed Part Two, go over the correct answers and discuss any questions that were answered incorrectly.

4. Distribute Worksheet 6-4B SAMPLE FEATURE. Instruct students to read the sample feature story and then answer the questions in Part Two.

5. Share and discuss student responses to the questions in Part Two.

6. Distribute Worksheet 6-4C WRITING A FEATURE STORY. Read and discuss the directions. When the students have completed their first draft, divide into critiquing groups and follow process writing steps for critiquing and revising.

Activity 5   HEADLINES

In a real newspaper, reporters rarely write their own headlines. These are created by copy editors, based on variable factors including space and page design. In school newspapers, however, the writers are often their own headline-makers. These are easy and fun to do, and student-reporters need learn only a few guidelines to engage in this interesting assignment.

PREWRITING ACTIVITIES

1. Copy onto the chalkboard several headlines from your daily newspaper, or use the ones below:

> Delays Loom on Route 80
> Few Voters Turn out for Runoff Election
> Boy, 4, Succumbs to Gunshot Wound
> Army Probes 'Copter Crash

2. Ask the students what these headlines have in common. Elicit the fact that each headline briefly states the main point of the story and that it is attention-grabbing.

3. Ask the students to identify the verbs used in these headlines. Elicit that each headline contains at least one verb and that present-tense, active verbs are used in each case.

4. Refer to the news stories written by the students for Activity 3. Ask students to create headlines for these stories, and write them on the chalkboard. For example, for the story about the Good Citizen Award, a headline might be "Eagle Scout Captures Good Citizen Award." A possible headline for the story about the Middle School computer club could be "New Middle School Club to Compute on Wednesdays." Insist that every headline suggested contain a verb, preferably an active verb.

5. Distribute Worksheet 6-5 WRITING HEADLINES. Read and discuss Part One.

6. Read the directions for Part Two. When students have completed their headlines, share and discuss them.

Activity 6   INTERVIEWS

Humans seem to have an insatiable curiosity about others of their species. Newspapers and magazines try to satisfy this innate voyeurism by means of the "personality profile." Often, these pieces are about well-known people. Many times, however, there is equal interest in ordinary, everyday folks, whose lives, characters, or experiences may be interesting or unusual in some way. In an interview, or personality profile, the writer tries to create a portrait in words. To be effective, it must be as complete, well-rounded, and detailed as possible.

The techniques for writing vivid profiles include the use of more descriptive details and direct quotes than are found in a news story. These details must help the reader visualize the subject's physical appearance, character, and background. Even more important than the actual writing, however, is the preparation and expertise of the reporter both before and during the actual interview. In this assignment, students will learn how to prepare for, conduct, and then write an interview.

PREWRITING ACTIVITIES

1. Ask the students how many of them enjoy reading interviews with movie or rock stars in newspapers or magazines. Most hands will shoot up (especially at the mention of "rock").

2. Suggest that an interview with ordinary people, any one in the class, for instance can also be interesting. Read to the class the interview piece from Worksheet 6-6A A STUDENT INTERVIEW. It appeared in an actual middle school newspaper.

3. Discuss this interview by asking the following questions:

   • How does the lead grab the reader's interest? (Quote, breeziness, and immediacy of manner)

   • What angle did the writer choose that makes the article more interesting? (Adam's unusual love of and interest in cars)

   • How do the direct quotes scattered throughout the article create interest? (The reader hears the subject's "voice.")

   • How does the writer paint a "word picture" of the subject? (Physical descriptions, details about his life, quotes)

   • Did the writer know anything about the subject before the interview? (Story told around school about his expertise with cars)

   • How do you think the writer prepared for this interview? (Asking other students about Adam, i.e., research, preparing a list of questions)

4. Distribute Worksheet 6-6A A STUDENT INTERVIEW. Read the directions. When students have completed the Worksheet, read and discuss their responses.

5. Tell the students that they will be paired up, and that each student in the pair will conduct an interview with the other, and then write it up. You can assign pairs or permit the students to choose their own. (Assigning usually works better.) Distribute Worksheet 6-6B PREPARING FOR AN INTERVIEW. Read and discuss Part One—Interviewing Guidelines. Read and discuss directions for Part Two—Your Question List. When completed, share and discuss some of the lists, and then let the students revise and/or add to their lists.

6. At this point, the students will meet in pairs and conduct their interviews.

7. Distribute Worksheet 6-6C WRITING THE INTERVIEW. Read and discuss the instructions.

8. When the students have completed their first drafts, divide into critiquing groups and follow process writing steps for critiquing and rewriting.

Activity 7 EDITORIALS ──────────────────

The area of journalism that middle grade and junior high youngsters seem to have the most trouble with is the concept of objectivity. They need constant reminders and editing to keep from injecting themselves and their opinions into news articles. This age group, however, flourishes when it comes to editorials. Here, they can give free rein to their propensity to put their own, personal thoughts into writing. They seem to have firm opinions on every subject ranging from school food to curriculum to personal relationships to society's current problems. With a minimum amount of encouragement, they are eager to share these ideas and try to convince others of their validity.

PREWRITING ACTIVITIES

1. Introduce a subject of current interest in the school or community. It can be something as local as a proposed change in curriculum, or a topic of national debate such as homelessness or TV violence. Choose a topic that will most likely evoke a difference of opinion. Ask for student opinions and conduct a brief discussion.

2. Point out that there are several different opinions right there in the classroom. Ask which students believe their conclusions to be the correct ones. Of course, all students who have entered the discussion will raise their hands. Tell them that the editorial page of a newspaper gives them the opportunity to state their ideas and convince others that they are correct.

3. Write on the chalkboard:

Editorial—An Opinion Essay

Ask the students how this might differ from a news story. Elicit that one of the essential differences is that a news story must be written objectively, while an editorial is an expression of personal opinion.

4. Distribute copies of an editorial you have clipped from a recent issue of a newspaper. A local publication is best since it is more likely to contain editorials of more immediate interest to your students. An editorial from a nationally oriented newspaper is fine if the subject impinges on the lives of your students (such as education, TV content, etc.) Read the editorial aloud.

5. Discuss the purpose of the sample editorial—to state an opinion and to influence the reader.

6. Discuss the structure of the editorial and analyze it on the chalkboard:

     Paragraph 1—statement of subject and opinion
     Paragraphs 2, 3 (and possibly more)—facts that support the writer's stand
     Last paragraph—summary

This will be more familiar to students than most journalism projects because it is the form they are accustomed to using in essays.

7. Distribute Worksheet 6-7A EDITORIALS. Read and discuss the sample editorial in Part One. (You may wish to point out that this editorial would have been improved by the addition of some facts.)

8. Read the directions for Part Two. When this has been completed, read and discuss answers.

9. Read the directions for Part Three. When the first draft has been completed, divide into groups and follow process writing procedures for critiquing and revising.

10. Distribute Worksheet 6-7B PERSUADE THEM YOU'RE RIGHT! Read and discuss the

directions. When the first draft has been completed, divide into groups and follow process writing procedures for critiquing and revising.

Activity 8 PRODUCING A SCHOOL NEWSPAPER ————————

Youngsters love to be involved in the production of a school newspaper. It can involve a lot of hard work, but is immensely rewarding for both teacher and students. Complete instructions for the production of a school newspaper would take up an entire book, but here are a few suggestions that may help you avoid some of the mistakes I have made.

Decide on scope. Will this be a newspaper for one class, a specific grade, or an entire school? The narrower the scope, the easier the production. A wider audience, however, offers more challenges and more opportunities for larger rewards, including development of writing skills, individual initiative, and responsibility.

Class or after-school activity? In the majority of schools, the newspaper is an extracurricular activity. This is the least desirable arrangement. It provides little or no opportunity for the students to learn correct journalistic procedures. The teacher/advisor can be driven crazy trying to collect and collate assignments from a staff that usually starts out huge and then keeps dwindling with no-shows and noncompleted articles. This arrangement works better at the high school level than for middle or primary grades, where it all too often ends up that the final work is done by a tiny group of dedicated writers. Certainly, some of the newspaper work will have to be done after school, but I strongly urge you to make every effort to have it produced as part of a journalism class or a journalism unit in reading or English classes, where there will be time for instruction and experimentation. This is true at all age levels.

Organization of staff. With a high school newspaper, the editors, if carefully chosen, can usually take the responsibility for most, if not all, of the editing. The younger the staff, however, the more work will have to be done by the teacher. Few sixth-grade students can be trusted with the responsibility of correcting spelling and grammar. The editors can, however, be given the responsibility of distributing and collecting assignments and designing the final copy. If enough students are available, a workable staff may consist of one or two editors, editors for special sections such as news, editorials, sports, reviews, features, etc., and reporters for each section. You might also want a typing or computer staff, depending on how the paper will be produced. Some of the older students will be capable of doing this. With the younger students, however, this will probably be done by the teacher or school secretary. If there is money involved (for example, if the newspaper is going to be sold rather than distributed free), you may wish to appoint a business manager, plus an advertising manager if you plan to use advertising. A box listing the names of staff members should appear on the editorial page.

The composition of a newspaper staff is essential to its success. Many students will sign up because they like the idea of being a reporter or the prestige of being on the school newspaper. Some of these Clark Kent types end up not only nonproductive themselves but disruptive in group activities. The advisor should try to know something about the students applying for the staff, either from his or her own experience or by questioning other teachers and administrators. Writing ability should not be the only criterion. Dependability and enthusiasm can be just as important.

The needs of the students should also be taken into consideration. High achievers will probably also be successful on a newspaper staff. There are other children, however, not so successful academically, who are dependable and have enough skill to make a contribution. For these youngsters, a chance to be on the newspaper staff can raise their status both in their own minds and in the eyes of their fellow students. Sometimes, they turn out to be tremendously creative in this area.

Production and design. The final copy of the newspaper can be as simple as a three-page typewritten class newsletter, or it can be a professional-looking school newspaper, produced by a computer equipped with desktop publishing software. The variations are as different as the scope and purpose of the publication, the size and ability of the staff, the place in the school curriculum, the time allotted, and the equipment and materials available. Whether simple or elaborate, the important thing is the writing. Is it clear, vivid, concise, and of interest to its intended readership? Of equal importance is its value to the staff. Working on a school newspaper should train students not only how to become better writers, but also how to work in a group, to meet deadlines, and to accept initiative and responsibility. Ideally, it should also provide them with fun, excitement, and increased self-esteem.

PLUNGING INTO THE NEWS

DIRECTIONS: Have you ever heard of famous monsters? There's the Loch Ness monster, and Bigfoot, to name just two.

Guess what? Someone has reported seeing a monster near your school. This is *big news*! Your local newspaper needs someone to write a news story about this amazing event. That someone is going to be *you*!

In the space below, draw a picture of the monster. Then, on the lines below, write a news story about this as it might appear in your newspaper. Tell what the monster looks like, who saw it, when it was seen, what the monster did, and what the principal of the school plans to do about it. (If you need more room, use the back of this Worksheet.)

HERE'S WHAT THE MONSTER LOOKS LIKE

HERE'S MY NEWS STORY

_____

_____

_____

_____

_____

_____

_____

_____

PLUNGING INTO THE NEWS

DIRECTIONS: You're going to pretend that a new exercise machine has just been invented. If it is used every day, it can actually make people *grow*! Isn't that exciting? It's also important news. And *you* are going to be the reporter who writes this story!

First, draw a picture of this amazing machine in the box. Then, on the lines below, write a news story about it. Tell what it looks like, who invented it and why, who has used it, and what the results have been. Also tell where people can get it and how much it will cost. And tell what the experts think. Will a person keep growing as long as the machine is used? What effect will this have on the world?

HERE'S A PICTURE OF THE MACHINE

HERE'S MY STORY

_____

_____

_____

_____

_____

_____

_____

_____

_____

_____

Name_____ Date_____

TEST

PLUNGING INTO THE NEWS

DIRECTIONS: What would it be like if a very famous person were to visit your school? What would this person think of your school? Why would they be there, and what would they do? What would they look like, and how would they be dressed? How would the kids act? What would some of them say and do? How would the principal and teachers act? What would some of them say and do?

This would be an exciting event. It would have to be reported in the newspapers. Guess who's going to be the reporter? You are! You're going to pretend that all this happened yesterday. Write a news story about it on the lines below. (If you need more room, use the back of this Worksheet.) One of the following people could be your surprising visitor (or any other famous person you wish to choose, real or imaginary).

the president of the United States

the Queen of England

Superman

a well-known baseball or football player

a famous actor or actress

Mickey Mouse

_____

_____

_____

_____

_____

_____

_____

_____

_____

_____

_____

_____

_____

PLUNGING INTO THE NEWS

DIRECTIONS: You are a reporter for your school paper. Someone has just given you a "hot tip"—two of your classmates have been chosen by NASA to participate in the first space voyage that will include students. You are going to write the news story about this exciting event. First, decide on the details by filling in the blanks in Part One. Then, write your news story below.

PART ONE: Fill in the blanks with any details you wish.

1. The names of the two who have been chosen for the space voyage are _____ and

_____.

2. There will be a total of _____ people in the crew. The others going along are _____

_____.

3. The name of the spaceship is _____. Its destination is _____. The trip will take

_____ months. They will travel _____ miles.

4. These two were chosen because _____

_____.

5. When told of their good luck, they said, "_____

_____." Their parents were very _____, and said, "_____."

PART TWO: Write your news story below. (Use the back of the Worksheet if you need more room.)

_____

_____

_____

_____

_____

_____

_____

_____

_____

_____

_____

Name_____   Date_____

SUMMARY AND QUESTION LEADS

PART ONE—DEFINITION: *Leads* are beginnings. In a newspaper article, a lead is the first sentence or sentences. Its purpose is to give the essential facts and make the reader want to read on. The lead should be as interesting as possible to grab the reader's attention.

Essential Elements: A lead usually answers the questions Who? What? When? Where? Only the simplest, most essential information is given in the lead. Details are provided later in the article.

PART TWO—TWO TYPES OF LEADS

1. *Summary Lead* states the facts. Following is an example of a summary lead: "At least four persons were killed and thirty injured in a traffic pileup on the East Expressway Saturday morning." Here is another example: "Municipal Court judge, Harrison Delray, yesterday ordered the City of New Orleans to fire 54 workers who received preferential treatment in a job competition last May."

2. *Question Lead* begins with a question to catch interest. Here is an example: "Why did they do it? A beautiful house in the small village of South Wentworth was destroyed last night by two teenage boys who were 'just looking for something exciting to do.'" Here is another question lead: "Have you lived before, in another body, at another time? Grant University yesterday announced the results of its three-year-long study on the claims of reincarnation."

PART THREE—NOW YOU WRITE: Below is information about a news event. Choose the facts you think are needed in the lead, and write *two* possible leads for this story. One should be a summary lead and the other a question lead. Both leads will be based on the following information:
1. *Who*—police report from Sergeant Chubb of 2nd precinct
2. *What*—break in; displays destroyed; windows broken; $550 worth of toys taken
3. *Where*—Kays, 25 Main Street, toy department
4. *When*—11:30 last night, found by J. Smith, manager.

WRITE YOUR SUMMARY LEAD HERE:_____

_____

_____

_____

_____

WRITE YOUR QUESTION LEAD HERE:_____

_____

_____

_____

_____

_____

QUOTATION AND PICTURE LEADS

PART ONE—DEFINITION: *Leads* are beginnings. In a newspaper article, the lead is the first sentence or sentences. Its purpose is to give the essential facts and make the reader want to read on. The lead should be as interesting as possible to grab the reader's attention.

Essential Elements: A lead usually answers the questions Who? What? When? Where? Only the simplest, most essential information is given in the lead. Details are provided later in the article.

PART TWO—TYPES OF LEADS

1. *Quotation Lead* begins with a quotation. "'Please arrest my son,' said the president of a large manufacturing company as he informed police of a crime committed this morning." Another example: "'I knew they were looking for me when I saw a helicopter overhead,' said twelve-year-old Mike Gold, who was rescued yesterday after being trapped for forty hours at the bottom of Greystone Gulch."

2. *Picture Lead* paints a word picture. "Curling black smoke and bright orange flames cast an eerie picture in a costly Halloween fire last night in the warehouse district of the city." Another example: "Oranges were scattered everywhere—on the highway, rolling down the grassy bank off the shoulder, and spilling from all sides of the overturned truck."

PART THREE—NOW YOU WRITE: Below is information about a news event. Choose the facts you think are most important and write two possible leads for this story. One should be a quotation lead and the other a picture lead. Write *only* the lead, not the whole story. Both leads should be based on the following facts:

1. *Who*—Little League Westside and Eastside All-Star teams
2. *What*—annual playoff game, won 5–4 by Eastside after a tie-breaking home run in overtime, hit by Sam Kutcher
3. *Where*—Eastside Field in New City
4. *When*—Saturday afternoon

WRITE YOUR QUOTATION LEAD HERE:_____

_____

_____

_____

_____

WRITE YOUR PICTURE LEAD HERE:_____

_____

_____

_____

_____

SHOCKING AND HUMOROUS LEADS

PART ONE—DEFINITION: *Leads* are beginnings. In a newspaper article, a lead is the first sentence or sentences. Its purpose is to give the essential facts and make the reader want to read on. The lead should be as interesting as possible to grab the reader's attention.

Essential Elements: A lead usually answers the questions Who? What? When? Where? Usually only the simplest, most essential information is given in the lead.

PART TWO—TYPES OF LEADS

1. *Humorous Lead* appeals to the reader's sense of humor. "Twenty-five-year-old Alice Rivers carried a torch for her boyfriend. The Riverdale resident was arrested yesterday on a charge of setting fire to three waterfront buildings. 'My boyfriend is a fireman,' she said. 'I like to watch him work.'" Another example; "'I guess there ain't no Santa Claus after all,' said the old derelict wistfully. He was arraigned in Municipal Court last night for possession of stolen goods after he tried to pawn a diamond ring he claimed to have found on Christmas Eve in the chimney of an abandoned building."

2. *Shocking Lead* shocks the reader into looking at the story. "'Jump! Jump!' the crowd shouted. The barefoot woman, holding a baby in her arms, stood on the roof of a burning building on High Street yesterday morning, staring in terror at the flames behind her and the hard pavement below." Another shocker: "The audience at the July 10th Bay City town meeting sat in stunned silence as they listened to their mayor of twenty years tearfully confess that he had stolen as much as thirty thousand dollars of township funds during his tenure."

PART THREE—NOW YOU WRITE: Below is information about a news event. Choose the facts you think are needed in the lead and write *two* possible leads for this story. One should be a humorous lead and the other a shocking lead. Both leads should be based on the following information:
1. *Who*—Jerry Whiteside, Student Council treasurer at Milford High School
2. *What*—resigned as treasurer after accusations that he had used student council funds to buy himself a motorcycle
3. *When*—last Friday
4. *Where*—at weekly meeting of the student council

WRITE YOUR HUMOROUS LEAD HERE:_____

_____

_____

_____

_____

WRITE YOUR SHOCKING LEAD HERE:_____

_____

_____

_____

_____

LIVELY LEADS

PART ONE: A *lead* tells the main points of a news story—Who? What? When? Where? But that is not its only purpose. A lead should also *sell* the article the way an ad sells a product. The lead should make the reader want to "buy the product," to become hooked enough on the story to want to continue reading. There are some simple techniques the writer can use to make the lead lively and exciting.

PART TWO—SOME EASY TECHNIQUES:

1. *Make the reader curious to know more.* Example: "Bank employees estimated the age of the tiny woman in black who stole $40,000 at gunpoint yesterday morning from the Springer National Bank to be between eighty and ninety." Or, " 'I don't know where I went wrong!' groaned the affluent Wall Street executive, as he watched police handcuff and lead away his fourteen-year-old son who is accused of being part of a gang that has been terrorizing and robbing subway riders in recent weeks."

2. *Use active verbs instead of passive ones.* Examples: "Mayor Frank R. Bean has been *jolted* out of office by an investigation by the district attorney's office that allegedly *reveals* widespread corruption at City Hall." "Passers-by *dodged* into nearby shops as gunfire *crackled* around them during a morning shootout between police and suspects yesterday on Main Street."

3. *Use striking, colorful details.* "A tiny woman in black" paints a more interesting picture than just "old woman." "A fast moving passenger train" is better than "the train." "The roar of splintering wood" is more striking than "The wood broke apart."

PART THREE—NOW YOU WRITE: The following leads could be improved by using some of the techniques described above. Rewrite each lead, changing passive verbs to active ones and using more colorful details. You can make up quotes and other lively details.

1. Student council officers met in the principal's office yesterday and asked for better service and food in the school cafeteria.

   REWRITE THIS LEAD HERE:_____

   _____

   _____

   _____

   _____

2. Eighth-grader Lara Forman says she is happy to have emerged unharmed after a confrontation with a burglar in the basement of her family home yesterday afternoon.

   REWRITE THIS LEAD HERE:_____

   _____

   _____

   _____

   _____

YOUR BEST LEADS

DIRECTIONS: Write a lead for each of the news stories below. You may *add* (make up) additional details or quotes, but you may not change any of the information given. Try to use different types of leads such as quotation leads, picture leads, question leads, etc. Make your leads lively by using *active* verbs and colorful details. WRITE ONLY THE LEAD, NOT THE WHOLE STORY.

News Story 1
WHO? James Fahs, of Seattle, Washington
WHAT? appointed principal of the South Street Middle School in North Salem
WHEN? announced yesterday by Sue Farrell, president of the North Salem Board of Education
WHERE? at the April Board meeting in the high school auditorium

WRITE YOUR LEAD HERE:_____

_____

_____

_____

_____

News Story 2
WHO? Matthew Holman, 12, seventh-grade student at Jefferson Junior High
WHAT? presented with Outstanding Youth of the Year award for rescuing a three-year-old girl who had fallen into the town pool where Matthew was swimming last July 10th.
WHEN? last Saturday
WHERE? at the fall luncheon of the Junior Chamber of Commerce, held at Arnoldi's Restaurant

WRITE YOUR LEAD HERE:_____

_____

_____

_____

_____

News Story 3
WHO? Jeni Kranz, 13, of Macon City
WHAT? winner of Poster of the Year contest sponsored by the National Wildlife Association
WHEN? announced January 13th by Samuel Rutgers, public relations director of the Association
WHERE? at the Association headquarters in Milwaukee

WRITE YOUR LEAD HERE:_____

_____

_____

_____

_____

THE NEWS STORY

PART ONE (READ AND STUDY): A reporter must know how to prepare news copy. Most newspaper stories contain a lead paragraph and the news body. The lead paragraph helps the reader decide if he or she wishes to read the story. The first few sentences should capture the reader's attention and interest. The lead may be startling or catchy and should tell what the story is about. Sometimes the lead includes a quotation from a person who was involved.

The body of the news story is written in *inverted pyramid* style technique, with short sentences and paragraphs. Facts are presented in order of importance. The most important facts are found in the first paragraph after the lead. The least important facts are found in the last paragraph. This arrangement allows readers to stop reading when they have gained all the information they need. Also, the editor may have to cut some of the less important facts at the end to fit the story into the paper.

A good news story follows these rules:

1. Write a lead to interest readers and grab their attention.

2. Decide which facts are most important and then pyramid the copy with the important facts at the beginning.

3. Use short sentence and paragraphs. (Most news stories contain two- and three-sentence paragraphs. Each paragraph should contain just one main topic.)

A simple news story should always answer the questions Who? What? When? Where? An in-depth story will also include Why? and How? The reader should find the answers to the first four questions very early in the story, preferably in the lead itself.

PART TWO: Answer the questions in the space provided.

1. What geometric shape does the news story follow?_____

_____

2. Why should the least important information appear at the end of the news story?_____

_____

3. What are the two purposes of the lead?_____

_____

4. What questions should be answered early in a news story?_____

_____/___

5. How many topics should there be in each paragraph?_____

_____

Name_____ Date_____

ANALYSIS OF A NEWS ARTICLE

DIRECTIONS: Read the news article you have been given, and then answer the questions below. When you have finished, attach your article to this Worksheet.

1. Copy the headline here _____

2. Tell about the story by filling in the four W's:

   WHO?_____

   WHAT?_____

   WHEN?_____

   WHERE?_____

3. If the story also answers the questions WHY? and HOW?, tell about it:

   WHY?_____

   HOW?_____

4. Are the four W's answered in the lead? _____ If not, which W is left out?_____

5. Which type of lead is used (summary, quotation, question, picture, humorous, other)?_____

6. Would you rate the lead as being excellent, good, satisfactory, or poor? Give at least one reason for

   your answer._____

7. If the editor cut out the last paragraph, what information would the reader never know? Is this information important for understanding this story?_____

   _____

   _____

8. If you were writing this story, would you change the order in which any of the details are presented? Which ones, and why?_____

   _____

9. Does the writer use any quotes? Who does he or she quote?

   _____

10. List below five words from the article that are vivid and strong?

   1. _____   4. _____

   2. _____   5. _____

   3. _____

Name_____ Date_____

WRITING A NEWS STORY

PART ONE (READ AND STUDY)

• PUT THE MOST IMPORTANT FACTS FIRST: Editors chop stories from the bottom to make them fit space. If you have something essential at the end of your story, it might be left out. News writers use the *inverted pyramid* style:

> Most important fact first;
> second most important
> fact next; and so
> on down to
> least im-
> portant
> fact

• MAKE IT READABLE: Use active verbs, vivid words, short sentences, and short paragraphs.

• USE THE FOUR W'S:
  WHO? Who is it about? Who said it?
  WHAT? What happened?
  WHERE? Where did it happen?
  WHEN? When did it happen?

• USE THE FIFTH W AND THE H, IF POSSIBLE:
  WHY? Why is it important? HOW? How did it happen?

• WRITE AN INTERESTING LEAD: Your lead should grab the reader's attention. It should also answer the four W's.

• NEVER USE *I* OR *ME*, OR YOUR OWN OPINION.

PART TWO: You are a reporter for the *River Falls News.* You are given the facts below and must write a news story. Use one of the following kinds of lead: summary, question, quotation, or picture. Your lead should answer the four W's. After the lead, be sure to tell the most important details first and the least important last. (You may make up additional details, such as descriptions of people or places, but you may not change any of the facts.) Write your first draft on a separate paper.

FACTS: Annual Good Citizen Award announced by Mayor Polly Titian of River Falls.
  Date of announcement: December 15th
  Name of winner: Good E. Tooshoos
  Details about winner: Senior at River Falls High School, age 17, son of Mr. and Mrs. Fabian Tooshoos, of 17 Memory Lane. Winner is an Eagle scout, president of senior class, star quarterback and captain of football team, member of Junior Chamber of Commerce and Future Doctors Club, will be attending Harvard University next year on full scholarship. Last month, ran into a burning building and single-handedly saved the lives of nine people by carrying them out of the burning house one at a time.
  Award will be presented at a gala dinner at the River Falls Country Club on January 15.

WRITE ANOTHER NEWS STORY

PART ONE: This assignment will involve writing a story for a school newspaper. The rules for news writing for a school publication are no different from the rules for a major newspaper.

1. Use an interesting lead that grabs the reader's attention.

2. Be sure your lead and your story answer the questions Who? What? When? Where? In your story also try, if possible, to answer Why? and How?.

3. Use the *inverted pyramid* style—most important facts first, least important details at the end.

4. Use vivid, exact words, active verbs, and short sentences and paragraphs.

5. Never use *I* or *me*, or your own opinion.

PART TWO: Here are the facts for your news story:

• Middle School Computer Club held first meeting last Wednesday.

• Tara Corman elected president.

• Also elected: Alan Adams, vice-president; Billy Halliday, secretary; Jenna Hancock, treasurer.

• Club will meet in Room 203 the first Wednesday of each month.

• President Corman said, "Spread the news, guys, we want new members."

• Nine people present at first meeting.

• Mrs. Data Bank, faculty adviser, said, "This is going to be a fun club."

• Dues: 50 cents monthly.

• Meeting began at 3:15 and lasted one hour.

• Plans made for a visit to a large computer store.

WRITE YOUR FIRST DRAFT BELOW (Use the back of this paper if you need more room):

_____

_____

_____

_____

_____

_____

_____

_____

_____

GUIDELINES FOR FEATURE WRITING

PART ONE—HOW TO WRITE A FEATURE STORY

1. The time element is not as important as in a news story. The subject can be of ongoing interest rather than a news event that has just occurred.

2. Feature writing is often more polished and more detailed since there is usually more time.

3. Feature writing usually demands more research and more interviewing than a regular news story.

4. The writer's own feelings and reactions can be included in a feature. It is even permissible to use the first person (*I* or *me*) occasionally in feature writing.

5. Leads can be more varied and creative than in straight news reporting. The answers to the questions Who? What? When? Where? Why? and How? do not have to appear until later in the story.

   A. The lead can be suspenseful, arousing the readers' curiosity and not letting them know the main point of the story until the second or third paragraph. For example, "There was a 'closed' sign on the door of the boardwalk hot dog stand. A gentle ocean breeze ruffled through the drawn shutters, causing them to clatter softly."

   B. The lead can be humorous. " 'Ghosts in the Middle School Auditorium? That's just an old myth.' Principal Jim Folson smiled and shook his head in disbelief. When asked, however, whether he had ever been alone in the auditorium at night, Folson shuffled uneasily and admitted that he had not."

PART TWO: Answer the questions below in the space provided.

1. How are feature story leads different from news story leads?_____

_____

_____

_____

2. Does a feature story usually contain more or less detailed description than a news article?

_____

_____

_____

3. Why do you think feature writing usually demands more research and more interviewing than

straight news writing?_____

_____

_____

SAMPLE FEATURE STORY

PART ONE: Read the feature story below:

JOURNALISM IN ACTION

Picture a group of students chewing on pencil ends, tearing at their hair and groaning, "It'll never be finished on time." That's what the staff of this newspaper usually looks like the day before a deadline. It's all part of putting together a newspaper. In case you've ever wondered, here's how it's done at this school.

First, the staff meets, and each person's assignments are discussed (news stories, sports, reviews, features, etc.). A deadline is set. If an assignment is not on time, it won't be in the paper.

After the deadline, editors and advisor meet to put together a "dummy," which is a rough outline of the newspaper. Articles are cut and pasted to fill pages, with no empty spaces. Headlines and design are made. You can always tell when an editor has been working on the dummy—he looks spaced-out.

When the dummy is finished, the staff types "masters." Masters are the final pages. These must be prepared carefully, with no mistakes. The editors and advisor check each master. Then they are run off on the copier in the office. The editors set out the stacks of pages, put them in order, and staple each complete newspaper. This makes for sore arms and hands.

Is it worth it? Listen to the staff. "I love it," exclaims editor Marisa Frank. "It's the most important thing I've done in school." Reporter Matt Capra remarks, "It's hard work, but loads of fun." Co-editor Corey Levi was not able to comment. He was too busy working on his editorial for the next issue.

PART TWO: Answer the questions in the space provided:

1. Identify the WHO, WHAT, WHEN, and WHERE of this story.

_____

   In which paragraph do you find this information?_____

2. List two ways that the writer may have researched this story. 1. _____

   2._____

3. How does the lead get the reader's interest?_____

_____

_____

_____

4. Why is this a feature, not a news story?_____

_____

_____

_____

Name_____   Date_____

WRITING A FEATURE STORY

DIRECTIONS: You are going to write a feature story based on the information below. If this were a real story to be printed in a real newspaper, you would have to research additional details. For the purpose of this assignment, you may make up any names, descriptions, and quotes you need to write the complete feature story.

Try to write an attention-grabbing lead. Try to make the lead humorous or suspenseful or unusual. Use active verbs and descriptions. Include a few quotes.

The headline (title) of this story is: A TOWN DIVIDED

FACTS—Residents of Middle Village are divided into two factions. One group wants to build an indoor pool for the town. The other side opposes it. Pool supporters include Mayor Art Callaway, and four of the six members of the Middle Village Board of Education. They point out that the nearest indoor pool is in Graham City, a forty-minute drive. They say it will be a safe, healthful place for kids to hang out after school during the winter months and will benefit all residents. The opposition is headed by Jason Skinner of Weller Road. He is president of a newly organized group called TARP (Taxpayers Against Robbing our Pockets). Skinner asks, "Where's the money coming from?" TARP is looking for support among property owners who Skinner claims will be paying for this "frill." They are circulating a petition to block this measure from being introduced to the City Council. TARP member Melanie Grail, who is also on the Board of Education, claims they already have 5,500 signatures. The disagreement has been going on since Mayor Callaway first proposed the pool a year ago, and both sides are getting more and more heated up as time goes on. TARP members complain that the pro-pool people are mostly non-property owners and don't pay taxes. The mayor's supporters call TARP "hard-hearted grouches who don't care about our children." Everyone in town seems to be on one side or another. Some close friends have become enemies over this issue, and at least one love affair has broken up. Art Foster, who lives on Oak Street, says, "We used to have dinner with the Metzgers once a week. Now we don't even speak to each other." Angie Carr supports TARP. She says, "My fiancé is pro-pool. We're about ready to call off the wedding."

BEGIN YOUR FEATURE HERE. YOU CAN USE THE BACK OF THIS PAPER TO COMPLETE IT.

_____

_____

_____

_____

_____

_____

_____

_____

_____

_____

HEADLINES

PART ONE: Headline writing is fun and creative. There are only a few rules you must follow.

1. Keep the headline short

2. Summarize the main point of the story briefly.

3. Use a verb, preferably an active, present-tense verb, in every headline.

PART TWO: Create a headline for each of these articles.

1. On Wednesday, March 4, eighth-graders from Watkins School went to Lincoln Center in New York to hear a concert on the evolution of the "scherzo." Scherzos include "jokes" on the audience written into the music by the composer.

   Leonard Slatkin, director of the St. Louis Symphony, conducted, and the New York Philharmonic performed works by Beethoven, Mozart, and Tchaikovsky.

   Student responses varied. Brian Sando called the concert "boring." Jenna Rich said, "It was okay." Bart Sloper found the music exciting.

   Write your headline here:_____

   _____

2. On December 19, Watkins School seventh-graders attended a program in the auditorium which was presented by Cecile Manheim. Mrs. Manheim told her story of her experiences during the Holocaust of World War II.

   Mrs. Manheim lived in Antwerp, Belgium. When her country was attacked, she had to flee from German soldiers. Her story was exciting, interesting, and kept her listeners in suspense. Mrs. Manheim came close to death six times during the war. She hid in people's homes and basements, and finally sought safety in Switzerland.

   Mrs. Manheim now resides in Seattle. She teaches a course on the Holocaust at the University of Washington, and also tells her story at programs such as this.

   Write your headline here:_____

   _____

3. Tony Aliengena, the eleven-year-old American trying to become the youngest person to fly around the world, left Iceland on Sunday, heading across the Atlantic Ocean to Norway.

   Tony said he was excited, but his father, Gary Aliengena, said, "He looks a little tired to me."

   Tony left for Norway at 11:10 A.M. The 1,150-mile flight to Norway was expected to take five or six hours. Forecasts called for considerable winds over the ocean.

   Write your headline here:_____ _____ __ _____ _ _ _____

   _____ _____ _____ __ _____ _____

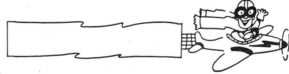

A STUDENT INTERVIEW

DIRECTIONS: The following interview appeared in a middle school newspaper. Read it, and answer the questions below.

EIGHTH-GRADER CARES ABOUT CARS

Eighth-grader Adam Fox is tall and thin. He has a ready smile and a habit of brushing his dark hair back from his eyes. Born in "the Big Apple," July 23, 1977, Adam has three brothers who "drive me crazy." He has no sisters, much to his relief.

Adam did not hesitate for a moment when asked about his hobbies. Among them are making car models, cars in general, trains, and playing badminton. Adam's interest in cars comes as no surprise. A story making the rounds at school is that Adam can walk up to a car blindfolded, feel the tires, and tell you what kind of car it is. Adam wouldn't confirm or deny that tale, but he did admit to an intense love of cars.

In school, Adam's favorite subjects are math, science, and reading. Although he is "not athletic," he does enjoy car racing (of course!), tennis, and soccer. His idols in life are Lee Iacocca, Garfield, and W.P. Chrysler.

The qualities that Adam looks for in a friend are "basic, but everyday good traits." He believes that "a friend has to be nice, able to understand things, helpful, and you should feel good around him."

Adam would like to attend Harvard when he finishes high school. Eventually, his ambition is to be chairman of Chrysler Corporation (what else?) or maybe start his own car company. One of his dreams is to own a limousine. "Basically," he says, "I want a good life, just like anyone else."

1. How does the writer grab your attention in the lead?

_____

2. What special angle or interest does the writer emphasize? _____

_____

   Underline four sentences in the article where this angle is used.

3. What other things about the subject do you know after reading this article?_____

_____

_____

_____

4. Circle descriptions that bring the subject to life.

PREPARING FOR AN INTERVIEW

PART ONE—INTERVIEWING GUIDELINES

1. Learn the background of the person being interviewed. (You can speak to his or her friends or teacher.)

2. Write out the questions in advance. Too many questions are better than too few. You can always omit from your story information that doesn't seem important, but too little information will result in a thin, boring story. For this interview, prepare at least fifteen questions.

3. *Never* ask questions that can be answered "yes" or "no." Word your questions so that they contain "what," "why," and "how." Ask some questions with depth, such as, "What are the biggest problems?" or "How will you go about doing this?" Then ask follow-up questions.

4. During the interview, take notes!!! Don't plan on remembering things, because you won't. In addition to the answers, write down information about your subject's physical appearance and mannerisms, and how he/she sounds or acts when answering a question. You may use a tape recorder, but you will still need notepaper to note descriptions and for back-up in case of "technical difficulties."

5. Include direct quotes. Check each quotation with the person being interviewed by reading it back at the end of the interview.

PART TWO—YOUR QUESTION LIST: Write your list of interview questions below. Prepare at least fifteen questions.

_____

_____

_____

_____

_____

_____

_____

_____

_____

_____

_____

_____

_____

_____

_____

_____

Name_____ Date_____

WRITING THE INTERVIEW

DIRECTIONS:

1. Study your interview notes. Decide in what order you will include the information.

2. Select the most unusual or interesting angle, and develop it for the lead.

3. The body of the interview story is just as important as the opening lead. The closing, too, should stand out and satisfy the reader.

4. Use direct quotes. Scatter them throughout the story.

5. Describe subject and background.

6. Choose words which will add color and life to the article. Use active verbs wherever possible.

7. Be sure to include an active verb in your headline.

WRITE YOUR HEADLINE HERE:_____

WRITE YOUR STORY HERE:_____

_____

_____

_____

_____

_____

_____

_____

_____

_____

_____

_____

_____

_____

_____

_____

_____

_____

EDITORIALS

PART ONE: An editorial must do two things:
1. State an opinion.
2. Present arguments to convince the reader.

Read the following editorial that appeared in a middle school newspaper. Be prepared to discuss how the writer tries to accomplish this double purpose.

Violence on television has grown through the years. Ever since *Miami Vice*, there have been more and more police shows and more deadly weapons. Children are affected by all this TV violence.

Violence not only occurs on nighttime TV, it also appears in cartoons. *Rambo* and *G.I. Joe* are just two examples of cartoons that contain a lot of violence. After children watch these, they want to play with toy guns and knives. What happened to *Sesame Street*?

Violence on television makes children have negative attitudes toward each other. Instead of playing tag or hide-and-seek, they want to play Rambo or play war.

When children are used to violence, they become less caring. They're so used to seeing people being beat up and killed, it doesn't faze them one bit. They also become more demanding of people.

Violence on TV should be reduced because it affects children's attitudes and the way they treat one another.

PART TWO: Answer the questions below:

1. What sentence in the first paragraph states the topic?

_____

2. State three facts the writer develops to prove his point._____

_____

_____

3. What is the writer's conclusion?_____

_____

_____

_____

4. Do you think this is a convincing editorial? Why or why not?_____

_____

_____

_____

PART THREE: Do you agree or disagree with the writer of this editorial? On a separate paper, write the first draft of an editorial expressing your own point of view. State your opinion in the first paragraph, and then present facts that will persuade the reader.

Name_____   Date_____

PERSUADE THEM YOU'RE RIGHT!

DIRECTIONS: Write an editorial that would be suitable for your school newspaper. You may choose any topic about which you feel strongly, or you can select one of the subjects below:

> Should there be a death penalty?
> Do schools really prepare you for life?
> Are there too many pressures on kids today?
> How can we keep drugs out of our school?
> Is there too much emphasis on sports in schools?
> Should billions be spent on space exploration?

Here are some suggestions for writing a good editorial:

1. Begin with a lively lead. State your main theme in the first paragraph.

2. Present *at least* three facts to support your opinion. State and elaborate on each fact in a separate paragraph.

3. Summarize and restate your theme in the final paragraph.

BEGIN THE FIRST DRAFT OF YOUR EDITORIAL BELOW.

_____

_____

_____

_____

_____

_____

_____

_____

_____

_____

_____

_____

_____

7
LETTERS

There is much talk about letter writing being a dying art in this era of rapid telecommunications. Yet, people still write letters to their friends and relatives who live far away. If one has a great deal to say, a first-class postage stamp is a lot easier on the purse than a half-hour long-distance call. Government, business, and industry, too, still rely to a great extent on written communications. In fact, one of the universal complaints voiced by businesspeople today is the inability of their young employees to compose a clear, well-written letter. There are many situations, both in business and in personal life, that can be handled only by written correspondence.

Writing effective letters is both a basic skill and an art. Even young children can begin to learn the satisfactions and rewards of a well-written letter. Once they see that such a skill can be useful to them now as well as later in life, it can be another area for providing practice and feedback in the process of writing. Since letter writing is such a personal form of expression, where the writer is intent on conveying his or her thoughts, feelings, or wishes to the reader, there is strong incentive for turning out clear and understandable prose.

The activities in this chapter will provide students with stimulating opportunities to exercise their writing skills in the form of letters. They will also be shown the relevancy of letter writing in their own lives and the ways in which well-written letters can be an advantage to them in many situations. Even the youngest students can be presented with instances where the ability to compose a clear, well-thought-out letter will bring about a desired result. Most of the exercises can be used interchangeably for grades four to eight, although the letters produced by the students will, of course, be appropriate to their own levels of writing. The process writing steps will help students learn to judge their own letters, and those of others. Some students may even end up agreeing with Anthony Trollope's perhaps exaggerated notion that "a pleasant letter I hold to be the pleasantest thing that this world has to give."

Activity 1   FRIENDLY LETTERS

Many young people resist writing letters because they are inexperienced in this art. They feel uncomfortable with the whole idea of letter writing and would prefer not to do it. The exercises and Worksheets in this section will demonstrate the correct form for a friendly (personal) letter, show models of both poor and well-written letters, and give the students practice in composing several different types of personal letters.

PREWRITING ACTIVITIES

1. Ask how many students have been away from home (perhaps at camp or with grandparents) and written to their parents or siblings. A few will probably respond.

2. Inquire how many have written to a relative who lives at a distance. A few may raise their hands.

142

3. Ask the students if they have had a friend who moved away with whom they correspond. Some may respond.

4. Discuss why letters are sometimes preferable to other means of communication, such as the telephone. Advantages that might be pointed out are cost, time to think about and compose thoughts more accurately, the fun of getting mail, the ability to read more than once a passage that might be important or pleasurable, and the advantage of having something in writing.

5. Distribute Worksheet 7-1A FRIENDLY LETTERS: GOOD AND BAD. Have the two letters in Part One read aloud. Discuss what is unsatisfactory about Letter A, and elicit the fact that it really says nothing. Point out the personal details that make Letter B better.

6. Read the directions for Part Two. When the students have completed the rewrite, have some of the letters read aloud for sharing and discussion. This is just a preliminary, warm-up exercise, and it is not necessary to go through the process writing steps.

7. Distribute Worksheet 7-1B FRIENDLY LETTERS: CORRECT FORM. Examine and discuss the various parts of the sample letter in Part One and how they are set up, including the heading, salutation (or greeting), body, closing, and signature. Point out the punctuation.

8. Read the directions for Part Two. Students should be able to answer all the questions in Part Two correctly before going on to the next Worksheet.

9. Distribute Worksheet 7-1C WRITE A FRIENDLY LETTER. Read and discuss the directions. When the students have completed their letters, divide into critiquing groups and go through the steps of process writing.

10. Distribute Worksheet 7-1D WRITE ANOTHER FRIENDLY LETTER. Follow same procedure as for Worksheet 7-1C.

Activity 2   THANK YOU LETTERS

Are thank you letters an endangered species? This is not an activity that children normally come to with spontaneity and enjoyment. It's much easier to pick up the telephone and get the uncomfortable chore over with quickly. And yet, a letter is so much more satisfying to the one who receives it. A written message can express appreciation in carefully chosen words. The recipient can share such a note with a partner, and can read it more than once, thus doubling or tripling the pleasure.

A thank you letter may be for something other than a present. A week-end stay at someone's home certainly deserves a note of appreciation in return. Sometimes one may wish to express thanks for a service performed. One of my favorite letters, reread with pleasure many times, was from a daughter who just wanted to thank me for being her mom and tell me that she didn't take my loving interest for granted. Something like that could never have been expressed as adequately in conversation. The dedication of teachers is usually accepted as a matter of course by their students. Every so often, however, a young man or woman may write to a former teacher, expressing appreciation for some help received or insight gained. What pleasure such letters bring!

If these activities will stimulate even a few children to acquire the habit of writing thank you letters, then they will be worthwhile.

PREWRITING ACTIVITIES

1. Ask the students how many of them have ever bought a present for someone else. Discuss the time and effort it took for them to decide on a gift, shop for it, wrap it, etc. Discuss how it makes them feel to know that the recipient really liked their present.

2. Ask the students how many of them like to write thank you letters. There will probably be widespread groaning. Refer back to the previous discussion, and point out the caring and effort it took for the giver to select and prepare the present, and the satisfaction he or she would get from knowing that the gift was appreciated. Ask why the students find writing a thank you letter such a chore. A discussion will probably bring out that they are never sure what to write. Tell them that this activity will make it much easier for them to write such letters.

3. Distribute Worksheet 7-2A THANKS A LOT. Read and discuss the directions and sample in Part One.

4. Read and discuss the directions for Part Two. When the Worksheet draft has been completed, divide in critiquing groups and follow process writing steps.

5. Distribute Worksheet 7-2B THANKS, BUT...Follow the same procedures as in Worksheet 7-2A.

6. OPTIONAL ACTIVITY—Here is an extra THANKS, BUT...activity that many students enjoy. When they have completed the letter for Worksheet 7-2B, let them compose a letter (never to be sent, of course) outlining their true feelings about the gift.

7. Distribute Worksheet 7-2C I JUST WANTED YOU TO KNOW. Follow the same procedures as for Worksheets 7-2A and 7-2B.

Activity 3   INVITATIONS

Occasions sometimes arise where young people need to send out invitations. Most boys and girls have a birthday party once a year, as well as other celebrations that they may wish to share. Many people purchase packages of invitations at the local greeting card store for this purpose, but others prefer to write their own personalized messages. This activity will help students learn how to design and write their own invitations.

PREWRITING ACTIVITIES

1. Ask the students how many of them have ever sent out party invitations. Let them relate the different occasions and types of invitations. Discuss the advantages and disadvantages of the various kinds of invitations mentioned.

2. Tell the students that in this activity they are going to write and design their own invitations rather than have to choose among those that are mass produced. Distribute Worksheet 7-3A INVITATIONS.

3. Read aloud the directions in Part One. Examine the sample invitations. Discuss the attributes that make the personally written letter more interesting and exciting, such as the detailed information that is given and the individual sound of the writer's own "voice" that comes through. (One student described this as, "I feel that I can almost hear him talking!") This would also be a good point at which to discuss the meaning of RSVP at the end of the information, and the responsibility of the recipient to acknowledge the invitation.

4. Read the directions for Part Two. Tell the students that this will be a draft and they will have the opportunity to revise their letters. Provide crayons or markers for those youngsters who may wish to illustrate or decorate their invitations. Fourth-, fifth-, and sixth-graders will be more likely to want to do this than the older students.

5. When the letters have been completed, divide into small groups and follow process writing steps for critiquing and revising.

6. If it fits in with your curriculum, this would be a wonderful time for the entire class to write actual invitations for a specific occasion, such as a school activity to which parents are invited or a class presentation to which other classes are invited. This activity can also be tied in with holidays for which usable invitations can be prepared, such as Valentine or Halloween parties, Memorial Day cookouts, end-of-school celebrations, etc.

7. Distribute Worksheet 7-3B "WEIRD" INVITATIONS. Read and discuss the directions. When letter drafts have been completed, divide into small groups and follow process writing steps for critiquing and revising.

Activity 4   PEN PAL FUN

Most youngsters get excited at the idea of having a pen pal, though they are sometimes intimidated by the challenge of finding one and then keeping up the correspondence. If their initial enthusiasm can be encouraged and nurtured, however, they will discover that the rewards of such a "literary" friendship can far outweigh the effort expended.

This activity will help your students get started on a pen pal project. It will guide them in the writing of that all-important first letter. This is often the greatest stumbling block, especially for those who lack confidence about their writing ability. The Worksheets accompanying this activity will lead them successfully through that initial hurdle. Once the contact has been established, it is then up to each student to continue the correspondence as long as he or she wishes. Sometimes the friendship is short-lived because the pen pals are not right for each other, in which case an alternative pen pal may be supplied. Often, they just get tired of writing. Occasionally, this activity can be the beginning of a satisfying long-distance friendship.

Even the teacher can get into the act. Many years ago, I began a correspondence with a pen pal in northern England, which lasted (with only occasional lapses) through the raising of our children, various political disagreements, and culminated in an actual meeting about fifteen years after that important first letter. We write to each other to this day and continue to share and compare the cultures and lifestyles of our respective countries. It has been a rewarding acquaintance and an opportunity to learn many things about another country.

Learning about other cultures or geographical areas is an exciting byproduct of such correspondence. Sometimes, when planning a pen pal exchange, the teacher may wish to take into consideration the possibility of coordinating this project with the social studies curriculum.

PREWRITING ACTIVITIES

1. This activity requires some advance planning. The teacher (or the class under the teacher's guidance) may opt to choose a school in another part of the country where each of your students will be a pen pal with a student in that school. Some schools have friendship exchanges with schools in a town of the same name in another state. There are international exchanges where students are matched up with pen pals of similar age and interests in other countries. Sometimes, it is possible to choose a specific country in which a student is interested. Here, too, pen pal exchanges between schools can be arranged.

   Organizations that supply pen pals are often listed in teachers' periodicals and references. Here are some you may wish to contact for this project:

   International Friendship League, Inc.
   22 Batterymarch
   Boston, MA 02109

   League of Friendship, Inc.
   P.O. Box 509
   Mt. Vernon, OH 43050

Student Letter Exchange
910 Fourth Street, S.E.
Austin, MN 55912

World Pen Pals
1690 Como Avenue
St. Paul, MN 55108

2. Prepare the students by involving them in the planning. Discussions can include where they would like their pen pals to live, what they would like to know about them, and what they will tell about their own lives.

3. It's nice to send snapshots with the first letters. If you tell the students about this in advance, they can have the photographs ready when it is time to write the letters.

4. Distribute Worksheet 7-4A PEN PAL INFO.

5. Read and discuss Worksheet directions. When the Worksheets have been completed, collect and analyze them to help you decide what type of pen pal project would be best for this class. Retain these Worksheets for possible use later in matching up pen pals.

6. Distribute Worksheet 7-4B PEN PAL FUN. Read and discuss the directions. This is a "loosening-up exercise." It is fun and easy to do and does not require process writing steps. It works best with students in grades four, five, and six. You may also find it helpful and motivating in some seventh- and eighth-grade classes.

7. Students who wish to do so may share their letters with the others by reading them aloud or by posting them in an appropriate place.

8. Distribute Worksheet 7-4C GETTING ACQUAINTED. Read and discuss the sample letter in Part One.

9. Read and discuss the directions for Part Two. When the letters have been completed, divide into small groups and follow process writing steps for critiquing and revising. (Although there is not likely to be much of a personal, secret nature in a first letter to a stranger, you might wish to forestall any unease by suggesting that it's okay for students to skip any sentences they would prefer not to share with the group.)

Activity 5 BUSINESS LETTERS

Youngsters in grades four through eight sometimes act astonished at the mention of business letters. It seems like something that their parents might need to know, but certainly not them. Yet, even young children may have the occasion to write business letters. Getting information for research papers, complaining about a defective product, and voicing an opinion for the "Letters to the Editor" section of a local newspaper are only a few of the uses to which students can put their knowledge of business letter writing. Once they learn the correct form for a business letter, they will find it of increasing advantage through the years. The recipients of a letter that is neatly and correctly set up and written in a clear, incisive manner are often more likely to give careful attention to the subject matter. The Worksheets in this activity will demonstrate the correct way to set up a business letter.

PREWRITING ACTIVITIES

1. Ask the students if they have ever had the occasion to write a business letter. Older classes will probably respond more actively to this question.

2. Tell the students that there are many occasions when knowing how to write a business letter can be an advantage to them. Offer some examples and try to elicit others from the students. Write these on the chalkboard. Your list might look something like this:

- writing a letter of complaint about a defective game

- getting information for a research paper (writing to government agencies, publishers, museums, etc.)

- a fan letter to a celebrity

- subscribing to a magazine

- writing a letter to the editor of a local newspaper

- ordering a replacement part for your computer

- applying for a summer job

3. Tell the students that their letters will make a better impression and possibly receive more careful reading if they use the correct form for a business letter. Distribute Worksheet 7-5A BUSINESS LETTER FORM. Read and discuss the business letter outline on the Worksheet. Point out that there are other styles and punctuation that can be used, but that they all include the parts shown on the sample. Read and discuss the descriptions of the various parts of the letter. Discuss the advantages of writing business letters on a typewriter or word processor, if available. Instruct the students to save this Worksheet and use it for reference when writing a business letter.

4. Distribute Worksheet 7-5B SETTING UP A BUSINESS LETTER. Using the sample letter in the previous Worksheet, students should be able to answer all the questions. Be certain that all answers on this Worksheet are correct before going on to another activity. The correct answers are as follows:
    1. Inside address
    2. Comma
    3. City, month
    4. Comma
    5. The person or company to whom the letter is written
    6. No
    7. Comma or colon
    8. No
    9. Body
    10. Halfway across
    11. First letter of first word
    12. Comma
    13. Enc.
    14. Inside address

Activity 6   RESEARCH BY MAIL

The usual sources for research, such as libraries and textbooks, sometimes do not provide sufficient information. The student who is able to compose a clearly written letter requesting information and/or materials (and who knows where to send such a request) is obviously in an advantageous position.

In this activity, students will study examples of letters requesting information, will compose their own letters of inquiry, and will be introduced to some helpful contact sources.

PREWRITING ACTIVITIES

1. Ask the students if they have ever had to write a research paper for which they were unable to locate all pertinent information. Elicit from the class, or suggest, sources to whom students can write requesting help, such as government agencies, museums, foreign embassies, etc.

2. On the chalkboard write several possible research topics. Next to each one, list several sources that might be contacted. Your list might look something like this:

A report on animals of the American northwest: U.S. Department of the Interior; Smithsonian Institution; American Museum of Natural History; National Geographic Society Magazine; Seattle Chamber of Commerce

A report on recent developments in aeronautics: National Air and Space Museum; NASA; Federal Aviation Administration; various commercial airlines.

A report on dentistry as a career: American Dental Association; a college of dentistry in your area; your family dentist; a professional dental publication.

3. Distribute Worksheet 7-6A RESEARCH BY MAIL. Read and discuss the sample letter in Part One. Point out the need to be clear and brief, while including all necessary information.

4. Read the directions for Part Two. When the students have completed their lists, share them with the class so that each student can add to his or her own list.

5. Distribute Worksheet 7-6B WRITE YOUR OWN RESEARCH LETTER. Read and discuss the directions. Be sure students understand they are to choose one of the sources indicated.

6. When the letters have been completed, divide into small groups and follow process writing steps for critiquing and revising.

7. Distribute Worksheet 7-6C WRITE A RESEARCH LETTER. Follow directions as in steps 5 and 6.

Activity 7   WRITING A FAN LETTER

Students love to write to famous people. They are even more thrilled when they get a reply. Of course, the more famous the subject, the less the chance of receiving any sort of personal response, but most youngsters will be quite satisfied with form letters, especially those that may be autographed.

This activity works best if the students are permitted to choose the recipients of their fan mail. The sports enthusiasts will want to write to their favorite pitcher, lineman, or goalie. Book lovers can contact authors whose work they enjoy. Almost all of the students will get excited at the idea of writing to a TV personality or a rock star. Gymnasts, skaters, and other Olympic athletes are favorite subjects. Some students' choices may surprise you. Their idols may turn out to be politicians (even the President is not out of bounds) or cartoonists. I once had a student who chose to write to the president of Chrysler Corporation as the man he most admired.

PREWRITING ACTIVITIES

1. Ask the students if they have ever written a fan letter. If there are any positive responses, discuss the details—who they wrote to, why, whether they got a reply, etc.

2. Ask the students for the names of well-known people they admire. Write some of these on the chalkboard. Elicit names until you have a variety of backgrounds, including sports, TV, books, and music.

3. Distribute Worksheet 7-7A WRITING A FAN LETTER. Read and discuss the directions in Part One.

4. Read and discuss the sample letter. Point out the specifics that make it good communication.

5. Read and discuss the directions in Part Two. Distribute Worksheet 7-7B WHERE TO WRITE, and direct students to the appropriate lists of addresses. If a student requires an address not on the list, direct him or her to a resource where it can be found.

6. When the first draft of the letters has been completed, divide into small groups and follow critiquing and revising steps of the process method.

7. When the final copies have been completed, distribute envelopes (or have students bring them in). Read and discuss the directions for addressing envelopes in Part Two of Worksheet 7-7B, and help students address envelopes and prepare their letters for mailing.

8. Distribute Worksheet 7-7C ANOTHER CELEBRITY LETTER. Read and discuss the directions.

9. When the first drafts have been completed, divide into groups and follow process writing steps.

10. Following completion of final copy, refer students to Worksheet 7-7B for addresses and envelope preparation.

Activity 8 PEN POWER

Most people, adults and children alike, fail to utilize the power of the written word to make known their opinions and needs, and to wield influence and bring about change.

The staff of any elected or appointed official can attest to the careful attention given to letters from the electorate, even messages from potential future voters such as children. Newspapers editors are well aware of the popularity of "Letters to the Editor" columns, and their effectiveness as vehicles for the expression of community concerns. Most of these missives are written by adults but, from time to time, a letter will appear written by secondary or even primary student presenting a school or community issue from the viewpoint of a young person. The fact that there are not more of these student letters may indicate the receipt of letters too poorly written to print, or may be the result of a lack of interest on the part of the young. This seeming uninterest may stem from ignorance that youngsters have the right or knowledge to express their views publicly. This letter-writing activity should, at least, provide students with an awareness of possibilities for their written intervention in the public sector and with the skills to carry it out.

PREWRITING ACTIVITIES

1. Write the following sentence on the chalkboard:

   The pen is mightier than the sword.

   Discuss the meaning of this sentence with the students. Elicit examples of instances where the written word has proven to be powerful. Possible examples are the American Declaration of Independence and the French Declaration of the Rights of Man, Salman Rushdie's *Satanic Verses*, spiritual writings such as the Bible and the Koran, etc. Perhaps there is some issue in your community that has been sparked or expanded by a local newspaper.

2. Discuss how ordinary citizens can influence events through writing. Write these methods on the chalkboard. These may include "Letters to the Editor" columns in newspapers, writing to members of the school board regarding school problems, letters to local, state, and national officials.

3. Tell the students that they, too, can influence events. Elicit student opinions on several current areas of local or national concern.

4. Distribute Worksheet 7-8A LETTERS TO THE EDITOR. Read and discuss the letter in Part One.

5. Read and discuss the directions for Part Two. Write names and addresses of school, local, or area newspapers on the chalkboard.

6. When the students have completed their letter drafts, divide into groups and follow process writing steps for critiquing and revising. Supply envelopes and mailing directions to those students who wish to send out their letters.

7. Distribute Worksheet 7-8B DEAR MR. PRESIDENT. Read and discuss Part One. (Explain that "Hon." in the address is the abbreviation for "Honorable" and is the correct form of address for a member of Congress.)

8. Read and discuss the directions for Part Two. When the letter drafts have been completed, divide into groups and follow process writing steps for critiquing and revising. Supply envelopes and mailing directions to those students who wish to send out their letters.

9. These activities should be followed up by sharing any responses, such as the printing of a student letter in the newspaper or a reply from a government official. Thus, students who have not actually mailed their own letters or who have received no response can see that letter writing can achieve results.

Activity 9   LETTERS OF COMPLAINT

Here is an activity to which everyone can relate. We've all purchased items that didn't work once we got them home, or fell apart after an indecently short period of time. Complaints are sometimes so rambling and incoherent that they are ignored, but a well-written letter that is brief, clearly states the facts, and specifically outlines the requested action can often achieve miraculous results.

PREWRITING ACTIVITIES

1. Ask the students if they have ever purchased or received a toy, game, or other item that didn't work. Most students will be able to relate at least one horror story of missing parts, pieces bent out of shape, incorrect screws or attachments, or inoperative motors.

2. Discuss what remedies are available and elicit or suggest a letter of complaint.

3. Distribute Worksheet 7-9A SAMPLE COMPLAINT LETTER. Read the sample letter on the Worksheet. Discuss and write on the chalkboard the three things that a letter of complaint should do:
   1. Explain the reason for writing.
   2. State the important facts.
   3. Tell exactly what remedy you want.
   Discuss how the sample letter handles these three components.

4. Distribute Worksheet 7-9B FILL-IN COMPLAINT. Read and discuss the directions. (This is a simple letter, already structured for the students, where all they have to do is fill in the blanks. It is fun for them to do and, at the same time, gives them practice in structuring a letter of complaint.) Read some of the completed letters aloud.

5. Distribute Worksheet 7-9C WRITE YOUR COMPLAINT. Read and discuss the directions. When the first draft has been completed, divide the class into small groups and follow process writing steps for critiquing and revising.

Activity 10 APPLYING FOR A JOB

Most students below high-school age do not seek the sort of jobs that require letters of application. Sometimes, however, such a letter is necessary, and it is certainly to a young person's advantage to learn early how to write the sort of applications that will eventually meet with success in the job market. Some seventh- and eighth-graders are beginning to look for summer jobs, and even sixth-graders often serve as baby sitters or "mother's helpers." Even students seeking volunteer positions may find it helpful to begin their search by writing letters. (You may find that this activity is not relevant to fourth- and fifth-graders.)

PREWRITING ACTIVITIES

1. Ask the students if they have ever done a job or performed a service for which they were paid. Discuss how they obtained these jobs. You will probably be able to develop the fact that, for the most part, they did not have to face much competition for this work.

2. Point out that there are some jobs where students must face competition with others, and the ability to present oneself well in a letter might make the difference between being chosen for the position or seeing it go to someone else. If you know of an incident where this has occurred, relate it, or tell about the thirteen-year-old girl who heard about a wonderful opportunity to spend the summer at an exclusive resort as a mother's helper. She put off doing anything about it for a while and then finally called the family, only to discover that they had received an interesting letter from another girl, had scheduled an interview, and were fairly sure they had found the right person for the job.

3. Distribute Worksheet 7-10A SAMPLE LETTERS. Read aloud both letters in Part One. Discuss why Letter A is poor (not enough information about applicant's qualifications as they pertain to this particular job, lack of references, arrogant tone) and what there is about Letter B that would make a prospective employer think well of the writer (pleasant, courteous tone, clear statement of pertinent qualifications and experience, references, willing attitude).

4. Distribute Worksheet 7-10B APPLYING FOR A JOB. Read and discuss the directions. When the first drafts have been completed, divide into small groups and follow process writing steps for critiquing and revising.

FRIENDLY LETTERS: GOOD AND BAD

PART ONE: Compare the two letters below. Which one is a better letter? Why?

LETTER A

Dear Steve,

   How's it going with you? I'm fine. Write soon.

                              Your friend,
                              Pete

LETTER B

Dear Steve,

   Things aren't the same on the block since you moved away. When the guys get together for a game, we really need you at shortstop. I miss walking to school with you, too. Remember all the fun we used to have? At least you're lucky that you didn't have to take the killer test in Mr. Cally's class.

   How do you like your new town and school? Write soon.

                              Your friend,
                              Pete

PART TWO: The letter below doesn't really say anything about the writer's day at school. Rewrite it on the lines provided. Make it more meaningful by giving details (real or imagined) about your own day at school.

Dear Mom,

   How are you? I'm busy at school. See you later.

                    Love,

Dear Mom, _____

_____

_____

_____

_____

_____

Name_____   Date_____

FRIENDLY LETTERS: CORRECT FORM

PART ONE: A friendly, or personal letter is the sort that you might write to a friend, relative, or acquaintance. The sample letter below shows the correct form for this type of letter.

(heading)   215 Elmsford Road

                   Caledonia, NJ 07498

                   October 9, 1990

Dear Pete,   (salutation)

   Thanks for your letter. It's nice to know that the old gang hasn't forgotten me.

   I really miss you guys. Even Cally's test doesn't sound so bad to me. The kids here don't seem that friendly. So far, I've made only one friend. His name is Philip. He's okay, but we don't like the same things. I think that maybe he's been nice to me only because the other kids don't like him. He lives on the next block so we walk home from school together, but it's not like when you and I used to laugh the whole time. He doesn't even like baseball!

   The best thing here is our new house. It's really neat. And you should see my room. It's huge! Mom's letting me fix it up the way I want. I wish you could see all the baseball posters on the walls.

   Write soon.

(body)

                          (closing)   Your friend,
                          (signature) Steve

PART TWO: Answer the questions below.

1. On what part of the page is the heading written?

_____

2. How many lines are in the heading?_____

3. What do the first two lines of the heading contain?

_____

4. What is indicated in the third line of the heading?

_____

5. Where does the salutation begin? What punctuation follows?

_____

6. What is the main part of the letter called?_____

7. Where is the closing written? What punctuation follows?

_____

Name_____   Date_____

WRITE A FRIENDLY LETTER

DIRECTIONS: Write a friendly letter. Your message can be made up or it can be true. You can write to an imaginary person or to a real one. You may choose one of the situations below, or make up your own. BE SURE TO USE THE CORRECT FORM FOR A FRIENDLY LETTER. Refer to the sample letter on Worksheet 7-1B if you need help remembering how to place the parts of a friendly letter. (This will be a first draft. You will be able to revise later.)

1. Write a letter to a grandparent or other relative describing what has been happening at home and in school.

2. Write a letter to a friend who has moved away, telling them all the things going on at school and in the neighborhood.

3. Write a letter to your mother or father at work, describing all the activities that take place while they are gone.

4. Write a letter to a pretend "fairy godmother" stating all the wishes you would like to have come true.

WRITE YOUR LETTER BELOW. BEGIN THE HEADING AT THE UPPER RIGHT.

WRITE ANOTHER FRIENDLY LETTER

DIRECTIONS: You can use some creative imagination when writing this friendly letter. You are going to pretend that you are in one of the situations below. Write a letter, making up as many details as you need. Be sure to use the correct form for a friendly letter. Refer to the sample letter on Worksheet 7-1B, if necessary.

1. You are spending the summer at Camp Ohbehaha. It is your second day there. You hate it. Your bunk is disgusting. Your bunkmates are all nerds. Your counselors treat you as though you are in the army. Worst of all is the junk they call food. Write a letter to your parents. Try to persuade them that they must come and take you home immediately.

2. You have been kidnapped by a gang of tough criminals, and are being held captive in an abandoned building in the city. You must write a letter to your parents, persuading them to pay the ransom demanded.

3. Your best friend moved away two years ago, and you lost touch with each other. You have just found out where that person now lives. Write a letter telling what has happened to you in the past two years, and saying why you think it would be a good idea to keep in touch.

WRITE YOUR LETTER BELOW. BEGIN THE HEADING AT THE UPPER RIGHT.

_____

_____

_____

_____

_____

_____

_____

_____

_____

_____

_____

_____

_____

_____

_____

_____

_____

_____

THANKS A LOT

PART ONE: When someone gives you a gift, they try to choose something you will like. The least you can do is offer them the pleasure of a written "thank you." It's easy, and doesn't take much time. There is no set rule you must follow. Be yourself and tell them what you feel. Say something about the gift to let them know you appreciate that particular item. Here is an example of a "thank you" letter. It is effective because it expresses the writer's real feelings.

12 Loree Road
Douglas, NH 11456
September 5, 1989

Dear Aunt Alice and Uncle Hank,

I was surprised and happy to get the beautiful jacket you sent for my birthday. It fits just right. How did you know that blue is my favorite color this year? The package came less than a week ago, and I've already worn the jacket three times. It goes with almost all my new skirts and jeans.

I wish you could have been here for my birthday. I had a great party, with terrific pizza. Thank you for thinking of me.

Love,
Susan

PART TWO: Now, you are going to write a "thank you" letter. You may choose one of the situations below, or one of your own. Be sure to use the correct form for a friendly letter.

1. Your grandparents have sent you a new video game for your birthday.

2. Your uncle has sent you a sweater for Christmas or Chanukah.

3. A neighbor has sent you the latest album from your favorite rock group for your birthday.

4. You have just spent the weekend at your grandparents' home.

WRITE YOUR FIRST DRAFT HERE. BEGIN THE HEADING AT THE UPPER RIGHT.

_____

_____

_____

_____

_____

_____

_____

THANK YOU, BUT...

PART ONE: It's hard to write a thank you letter for a gift you hate. It could be something you already have, or something you don't like or cannot use. What can you write? You don't want to tell your true feelings, but you don't want to lie, either. It helps if you can put aside your own disappointment and think about the giver's effort to make you happy. Your letter will be truthful and appreciative if you concentrate on the thought behind the gift, as in this letter.

---

5 Alpine Way
Nottingham, WI 85476
January 20, 1990

Dear Aunt Louise,

    Thank you so much for the purple umbrella. It was so nice of you to remember that yesterday was my birthday. I know how busy you are this time of the year.

Love,
Samantha

PART TWO: Write a thank you letter for one of the following:

1. a toy or game suitable for someone three years younger

2. a shirt you wouldn't be caught dead in

3. a cassette you already own

4. a book you read last year

5. the ugliest scarf (or tie) in the whole world

Your letter can be addressed to a relative, neighbor, friend, etc. Remember to concentrate on the thought behind the gift. Begin your letter here. Use correct form for a friendly letter.

_____

_____

_____

_____

_____

_____

_____

_____

Name_____   Date_____

I JUST WANTED YOU TO KNOW

A mother once received a letter from her daughter that said, in part:

"I just wanted you to know how glad I am that you are my Mom. You're really special to me, and I love you a lot. I know it doesn't seem like it a lot of the time, but the truth is that I hope I'll be like you when I'm older."

You can imagine how that mom cherishes that letter. What about people who have made a difference in your life? Do you always let them know how you feel? If not, now is your chance to do so in writing so that they can always have it to look at when they need cheering up.

Think of somebody who has done something nice for you. It could be your mom or dad who have loved and cared for you. Perhaps you have grandparents who are good to you, or an aunt or uncle with whom you have a special relationship. How about a good longtime friend—have you ever let that person know how much their friendship means to you? Was there a teacher who led you to develop some special ability or helped you see yourself in positive ways? Is there someone with whom you spent a wonderful vacation? Perhaps you'd just like to thank someone for being a super role model. Express your thanks in writing to one of these people. Write your letter below, using the correct form for a friendly letter.

_____

_____

_____

_____

_____

_____

_____

_____

_____

_____

_____

_____

_____

_____

_____

_____

(7-2C)

INVITATIONS

PART ONE: Read and compare these two invitations:

A

Come to a birthday party
FOR: Pete Rogoff
DATE: January 3
TIME: 9 a.m.
PLACE: 450 West Street
RSVP: 555-0067
(Bring ice skates)

B

450 West Street
Alsburg, PA 19857
December 19, 1990

Dear Pat,
    Guess what? My parents are letting
me have an ice skating party for my
birthday this year. We're going to meet
at my house at 9 a.m. Mom and Dad will
drive us to Ice World Rink, and we can
skate there all morning. Then, we're
going to Burger King for lunch. We'll get
home about 2:30 p.m.
    My folks say I can invite my three
best friends. I hope you can come.
                        Your friend,
                        Pete

RSVP—555-0067

Isn't Letter B the invitation you would prefer to receive? It seems so much more personal and individual. Doesn't it make you feel as though you are really wanted?

PART TWO: Write a letter of invitation to a friend. You can make up the occasion, date, place, and details. It can be a birthday party with a rock music theme, a Halloween party where everyone wears costumes, an end-of-term barbecue in your backyard, or even a real party that you are planning to give soon. Use the correct form for a friendly letter, and be sure to include an RSVP.

_____

_____

_____

_____

_____

_____

_____

_____

_____

"WEIRD" INVITATIONS

DIRECTIONS: Wouldn't it be fun to write an invitation to a really weird activity, such as a party for chocolate lovers, or a seat on the first manned spaceship to Mars? You can choose one of these special occasions, or one of those listed below, or you can make up a wild activity of your own. It can be real or imaginary. Here are some other possibilities:

    a computer-game championship party
    a neighborhood treasure hunt
    a party in the rain
    a membership in the "Save Our Cockroaches" club
    a dragon party
    a dinosaur convention
    a space-age costume party
    a robot convention

Write your letter below. Be sure to use correct form for a friendly letter. Include an RSVP.

_____

_____

_____

_____

_____

_____

_____

_____

_____

_____

_____

_____

_____

PEN PAL INFO

DIRECTIONS: A stranger can quickly become a friend if that stranger is a pen pal. It's fun to exchange letters with someone your own age who lives in another city or country. You can learn a lot about a person from their letters, and it's exciting to compare customs and lifestyles, such as the way you celebrate holidays, school subjects and hours, food, clothing, and lots of other things.

Answer the following questions carefully. Your answers will help get you matched up with the right pen pal for you, one who just might become a lifelong friend.

1. Write your home address here_____

2. Write your age and grade in school here_____

3. Do you prefer a boy or girl as a pen pal?_____

4. If you have brothers or sisters, write their names and ages here

_____

5. What school subjects do you like best?_____

6. What are your least favorite school subjects?_____

7. What pets do you have, if any?_____

8. Do you prefer having lots of friends, or a few good ones?_____

9. Do you often like to be alone? _____. If your answer is yes, tell what you enjoy doing by yourself

10. Do you like to read? _____. What books do you like?_____

_____

11. Do you like to watch TV? _____. What are your favorite TV shows?_____

12. Do you like movies? _____. What are your favorite movies? _____

_____

13. What sports do you enjoy playing or watching?_____

_____

14. What do you usually do after school?_____

15. What kind of pen pal would you like?_____

_____

_____

_____

Name_____   Date_____

PEN PAL FUN

DIRECTIONS: Fill in the blanks in the letter below. When you have finished, you will have an example of the sort of first letter you might wish to write to a pen pal.

_____
(your street address)

_____
(your town, state, and zip)

_____
(today's date)

Dear Sean,

My name is _____. I am _____ years old and in _____ grade at the _____ school in _____. I would like to be your pen pal.

The town in which I live is _____ and _____. Some interesting things to see around here are _____ and _____. I live in a _____ house/apartment. There are _____ people in my family. Besides me, there are _____, _____. I _____to _____ with my family.

My favorite after-school activity is _____. I'm also interested in _____, and I like to _____. My favorite foods are _____ and _____. When I grow up, I would like to be _____. I like friends who are _____and _____, and one person I really admire is _____.

I'd like to know all about you, and find out what it's like where you live. I hope you'll write soon.

Your friend-to-be (I hope)

_____
(Sign your name here)

(7-4B)

GETTING ACQUAINTED

PART ONE: Now that you have the name and address of a possible pen pal, it is time to write a first letter. Below is a sample letter that one student wrote to a pen pal:

24 Grant Street
Andover, NJ 07458
July 5, 1990

Dear Maria,

I'm very nervous about this letter, because I've never written to anyone before who lives in another country. I'm excited about becoming your pen pal.

I am 12 years old. In September, I will be going into seventh grade. Our school is closed during July and August. Do you have school in the summer? I like school pretty much, except for math, which always gives me trouble. My best subject is reading. Next year, I'll be taking Spanish. Maybe then I'll be able to write to you in your own language.

I live with my mom and my bratty little brother, Mike. My parents are divorced. I spend every other weekend with my dad. My best friend's name is Lara. She lives around the corner. We like to watch TV together and to play games. Our favorite game is Monopoly. We take gymnastics together twice a week. In August, we are both going to a gymnastics camp.

Please write to me soon, Maria, and tell me all about yourself. I hope we will be friends.

Your pen pal,
Bonnie

PART TWO: Write a letter to your pen pal in your own style, telling about yourself. Write your heading first in the upper right. Use the back of this paper if you need more room.

_____

_____

_____

_____

_____

_____

_____

_____

_____

_____

BUSINESS LETTER FORM

Below is one correct way to set up a business letter. (Other styles are sometimes used, but they all contain the parts shown here.)

	(Writer's street address) — (return
	(City, state, and zip) — address)
	(Current date) —
(inside address)	(Name of person or company to whom you are writing)
	(Their street address)
	(City, state, and zip)
(salutation)	Dear Sir or Madam:
(body)	Your message will appear here. This is called the body of the letter. State your message clearly so that the person who reads it will understand your wishes.
	Yours truly, — (closing)
	(Sign your name here)
	Enc. (This indicates that you are enclosing something with your letter.)

1. In a business letter, the heading is called *the return address*. It is written in the upper right. There are three lines in the return address. The first shows your street address. The second line indicates the city or town, state, and zip code. Use the correct post office abbreviation for the state (NJ for New Jersey, CA for California, WI for Wisconsin, etc.). Do not abbreviate the city. The date is on the third line. *Do not abbreviate the month.*

2. The *inside address* usually contains three lines. The first line is the name of the person or company to whom you are writing. The second line indicates their street address. The third line shows the city, state, and zip code. The state may be abbreviated as described above. Each line begins at the left margin. Do not indent. (This is exactly the same as the address on the envelope.)

3. The *salutation* (or greeting) also begins at the left margin. It is followed by a comma (,) or a colon (:).

4. The *body* of the letter contains your message. You may indent at the beginning of each paragraph.

5. The *closing* begins halfway across the line at the same point as the *return address*. Only the first letter of the first word is capitalized. A comma (,) follows.

6. Your *signature* is written under the closing.

7. If you are enclosing anything with your letter, write *Enc.* at the bottom of your letter at the left margin.

8. Try to center your letter on the page. Use a typewriter or word processor, if possible.

Name_____   Date_____

SETTING UP A BUSINESS LETTER

Answer the questions below in the space provided. You can find all the information you need by referring to Worksheet 7-5A BUSINESS LETTER FORM.

1. Name one part of a business letter that does not appear in a friendly letter._____

2. What mark of punctuation appears after the name of the city in the return address?_____

3. Name two things in the return address that should not be abbreviated._____

4. What punctuation mark is used between the day and the year in the date?_____

5. Whose name and address appears in the inside address?

_____

6. Is the inside address indented?_____

7. Name two marks of punctuation that may be used after the salutation._____

8. Is the salutation indented?_____

9. What is the message part called?_____

10. At what point on the line does the closing begin?

_____

11. Which part of the closing is capitalized?_____

12. What mark of punctuation follows the closing?_____

13. What do you write to show that something is being enclosed with the letter?_____

14. Which part of the letter appears exactly the same on the envelope?_____

Name_____   Date_____

RESEARCH BY MAIL

PART ONE: Pete is doing a report on the history of railroads in the United States. He has written the following letter:

---

35 Well Street
Middletown, CT 06457
September 28, 1990

Union Pacific Railroad
1416 Dodge Street
Omaha, NE 68179

Dear Sir or Madam:

   I am doing a report on the history of railroads in the United States. Do you have any pamphlets and maps which would give me information on the early years of your railroad and also on recent developments?

   I would also appreciate receiving photographs of railroad equipment and of people who have been important in the development of your railroad.

   Thank you for any help you can give me.

Yours truly,

Pete Smith

PART TWO: Can you think of other places Pete could write to get information for his report? List them below (you don't need addresses—names are enough).

_____

_____

_____

_____

_____

_____

WRITE YOUR OWN RESEARCH LETTER

DIRECTIONS: You are preparing to write a report on the early years of radio broadcasting in the United States. Two possible sources of information are listed below. Choose one of them and write a letter asking for information. Be sure to use correct business letter form.

Broadcast Pioneers Library
1771 N St. NW
Washington, DC 20036

or

National Public Radio
2025 M Street NW
Washington, DC 20036

Write your letter here. Begin the return address in the upper right.

Name_____ Date_____

WRITE A RESEARCH LETTER

DIRECTIONS: You are preparing to write a report on the Cherokee tribe of American Indians. Two of the places you could write to for information are listed below. Choose one of them and write a letter. Tell about your project and ask for information and materials. Be sure to use correct business letter form.

Cherokee National Historical Society
Box 515, TSA-LA-GI
Tahlequah, OK 74464

or

American Museum of Natural History
Central Park W. at 79th Street
New York, NY 10024

Write your letter here. Begin your return address at the upper right.

_____

_____

_____

_____

_____

_____

_____

_____

_____

_____

_____

_____

_____

_____

_____

_____

_____

WRITING A FAN LETTER

PART ONE: Would you like to talk to your favorite TV personalities and tell them how much you admire them? How about the star pitcher on your hometown team? Wouldn't it be great if you could tell him how terrific you feel whenever he pitches the team to victory? And that rock album you listen to so often that it's wearing out—don't you think that group wants to know how much you love their music? The same is true for the author of that book you liked so much you couldn't put it down until you had finished it, or that movie star you wish you could be like.

You like someone to pat you on the back and say, "Good work!" when you've done a job well. Performers, athletes, writers, and other famous people love to hear from their fans, too. That's how they know that people appreciate their work. Some celebrities are too busy to answer all the letters they get, but others answer their fan mail faithfully. You're more likely to get a reply if you write an interesting, honest letter like the one below.

---

58 Maple Street
Haskell, NJ 07498
March 8, 1990

Mr. Rock Starr
ABC Records
55 East 59th Street
New York, NY 10036

Dear Rock,

Congratulations on your latest album, "Get Me!" I bought it last week and I've already worn it down because I play it so much. Sometimes, when I get depressed, I listen to your music and soon I feel happy again.

I love all your albums, but "Get Me!" is really the best ever! I hope you will keep on making albums forever. I would love to have an autographed picture, if that's possible. I would treasure it forever.

Your biggest fan,
Mike Grant

Note how the writer mentioned a specific work, and gave interesting details about his feelings about it.

PART TWO: On a separate sheet of paper, write the draft of a fan letter to someone you admire. Your teacher will give you a Worksheet containing lists of addresses. Choose the one that seems appropriate for your letter.

WHERE TO WRITE

Here are some addresses that may be helpful to you when writing to celebrities:

• **MAJOR TV NETWORKS**
  NBC-TV, 30 Rockefeller Plaza, New York, NY 10020
  ABC-TV, 1330 Avenue of the Americas, New York, NY 10019
  CBS-TV, 51 West 52nd Street, New York, NY 10009
  PBS, 425 L'Enfant Plaza SW, Washington, DC 20024
  (For local stations in your area, look in the Yellow Pages of the telephone book under Television Broadcasting.)

• **MUSIC:** Write to recording stars in care of the record company whose name and address appears on the album or cassette. Some major record producers are:
  A&M Records Inc., 1416 LaBrea Ave., Hollywood, CA 90028
  RCA Records, 30 Music Square W., Nashville, TN 37203
  CBS (Columbia) Records Inc., 51 W. 52nd Street, New York, NY 10009
  Warner Bros. Records Inc., 4000 Warner Blvd., Burbank, CA

• **SPORTS:** You can write your favorite athlete in care of the team. Look in your telephone book for the address.

• **AUTHORS:** Authors can be reached in care of the publishing company. The publisher's name and address is found on the copyright page at the front of the book.

• **MOVIES:** You can write to a film star in care of the studio that produces the movie. The producer's name often appears in newspaper ads. Here are some major studios:
  Columbia Pictures, Columbia Plaza, Burbank, CA 91505
  Disney Prod., 500 South Buena Vista St., Burbank, CA 91521
  Allied Artists, 9200 Sunset Blvd., Los Angeles, CA 90069
  20th Century Fox Corp., 10201 West Pico Boulevard, Los Angeles, CA 90064
  LucasFilm, 3855 Lankershim Blvd., N. Hollywood, CA 91604
  Paramount Pictures, 5451 Melrose St., Los Angeles, CA 90038

• **THE ENVELOPE:** The return address appears in the upper left. It has three lines, the first being the name of the writer, the second the writer's street address, and the third the city, state, and zip. The address of the person to whom you are writing begins in the center, about halfway down from the top. It matches the inside address in the letter.

```
Michael Davis
23 First Street
Sacramento, CA 19006

                    Mr. Rock Starr
                    A&M Records Inc.
                    1416 LaBrea Avenue
                    Hollywood, CA 90028
```

ANOTHER CELEBRITY LETTER

Choose another actor, athlete, writer, musician, or other famous person whom you admire. Write a letter to this celebrity. Tell why you admire him or her. Speak about how this person's accomplishments may have inspired you or brought you moments of pleasure. Personalize your letter by telling a little bit about yourself.

Write your draft on the lines below. Use correct form for a business letter. Refer to Worksheet 7-7B for help in finding the correct address.

LETTERS TO THE EDITOR

PART ONE: Do you have an opinion about problems in your community or in the world? You can make your ideas count by sending them to the "Letters to the Editor" column of a newspaper. Here is a letter that appeared in one newspaper:

> Dear Editor,
>   I am a seventh-grade student at Weston Middle School. My classmates and I were very upset at a recent editorial that appeared in your newspaper describing vandalism at Weston Park.
>   You made it appear as though all teenagers are destructive. This is not true. Most of us respect the law. We care a lot about Weston Park because we enjoy hanging out there. We hate the vandalism just as much as you do.
>   Your article suggested that all teenagers should be barred from the park. It is not fair to punish all of us for the actions of a few.
>   Yours truly,
>   *Marissa Newman*

The editor probably chose to print this letter because it concerned a problem of concern to the community, was clearly written, and expressed an important point of view. People are interested in the ideas of young people.

PART TWO: What do you think about what's going on in your school, your community, or the world? You are going to write a letter for the "Letters to the Editor" column of your school newspaper, or a local or area newspaper, expressing your opinion. Here are some possible topics:

1. Improving cafeteria service in your school

2. A dangerous situation that exists somewhere in your school or on the playground

3. A proposal for building an indoor town pool

4. How to make the streets of your city safer

5. How to handle the drug problem in your community

6. What the future of the space program should be

The first two topics would be appropriate for a school newspaper, if you have one. Topics 3, 4, and 5 should be directed to a local newspaper. Topic 6 could be used for any of the three. You may choose one of these subjects, or any other that appeals to you. Write the first draft of your letter on a separate paper, using correct business letter form. The inside address and salutation should follow this form:

> Editor
> Name of newspaper
> Name of school or street address
> City, state, and zip
> Dear Editor:
>   (The rest of the letter can follow the business letter format.)

Name_____ Date_____

DEAR MR. PRESIDENT

PART ONE: In a democracy, government officials are interested in the opinions of the citizens, even young ones. You have the right to write to the mayor of your city, your congressperson, the governor, even the President himself. Abraham Lincoln once received a letter from a young girl suggesting that he should grow a beard. Not only did he reply to her letter, he even followed her suggestion! Following is a letter that one young person wrote to his congressman:

---

289 Reservoir Road
Springfield, WI 08651
September 6, 1990

Hon. James Roe
House of Representatives
Washington, DC 20515

Dear Congressman Roe:

   Air pollution is a serious threat to our country. I am thirteen years old, and I am afraid that when I grow up, the air will not be fit to breathe.
   I hope that you will try to introduce and pass laws that will protect the quality of our air.

Yours truly,
David Deloroa

PART TWO: On a separate paper, write the first draft of a letter to an elected official, expressing your ideas. Below are some helpful addresses:

   The President, The White House, Washington, DC 20500
   Your U.S. Senator, Senate Office Building, Washington, DC 20515
   Your U.S. Congressperson, House of Representatives, Washington, DC 20515

If you write to local or state officials, your teacher will supply you with the correct addresses. Use correct business letter form, and state your position briefly and clearly.

SAMPLE COMPLAINT LETTER

Businesses get a great deal of mail. Busy employees may overlook or put aside letters that are unclear, confusing, and difficult to comprehend. If you are writing to complain about services or something you have bought, you will find your letter gets a better response if it is brief and clearly written. Your letter of complaint should make three clear statements. You should:

1. explain your reason for writing;

2. state the important facts;

3. tell exactly what remedy you want.

Your letter might look something like this:

---

415 Eagleton Drive
Seattle, WA 90087
January 6, 1990

Johnson Hobby Company
Benson Building
Chicago, IL 60611

Dear Sir or Madam:

I recently purchased your motorized truck, model #53-A. When I began to use it, the windshield wipers fell off, the wheels loosened up and wobbled, the gear shift became stuck in reverse, and the motor kept turning itself off after less than one minute of operation.

I am returning the truck to you in a separate package. Please send one that works properly, or return the purchase price of $8.98.

Yours truly,

Notice how the writer of this letter handles the three things that a complaint letter must contain. He explains his reason for writing (he bought a product that didn't work). He lists exactly what was wrong. Last, he clearly states that he wants a new, perfect truck, or his money back.

Name_____   Date_____

FILL-IN COMPLAINT LETTER

DIRECTIONS: Complete the following letter of complaint by filling in the blanks.

_____
(Write your street address here)

_____
(Your city, state, zip)

_____
(Today's date)

Value Catalog Co.
Box 3465
Grand Rapids, MI 79056
Dear Sir or Madam:

   I recently ordered an invisible writing kit from your _____ catalog.

The ad appeared on page _____, catalog number _____.

   The kit arrived in _____ condition. The bottle of ink was

_____, the special pens were _____, and the _____was

missing. In addition, there were _____

_____.

   I am very _____ about this, because I had planned to give the kit as a

_____ gift to my _____. Would you be able to send me a new

_____ by _____? If you cannot _____ it by that date,

please return the purchase price of _____.

   I hope you will _____ this matter promptly.

Yours truly,

_____
(Sign your name here)

WRITE YOUR COMPLAINT

DIRECTIONS: You recently ordered two computer games for your Apple IIc computer from the Super Software Catalog Co., Box 7997, Chicago, IL 80976. The two games are "Heroes of the Universe" (catalog number 37D; cost $12.50) and "Knights in Armor" (catalog number 42C; cost $14.90). The first game seems to work perfectly, but "Knights in Armor" arrived in a ripped package and does not work at all.

You are going to return "Knights in Armor" and write a letter of complaint to the Super Software Catalog, asking for a new disk or your money back. In your letter, be sure to explain your reason for writing, state the important facts, and tell exactly what remedy you want.

Write your letter below, using correct business form.

_____

_____

_____

_____

_____

_____

_____

_____

_____

_____

_____

_____

_____

_____

_____

_____

_____

_____

_____

SAMPLE LETTERS

PART ONE: A local newspaper printed a notice that they were looking for carriers to deliver their Sunday papers. They received the following two letters. If you were in charge of the carriers, which writer would you call for an interview? Why?

LETTER A:

November 5, 1990

Dear Star-Times:

   I saw your ad for newspaper carriers. I think I might want that job if it pays a good salary. I can work most Sundays except when my family goes away for the weekend.

   I live near your office, so I'll stop by to see you next Wednesday afternoon to talk about the job.

Yours truly,

LETTER B:

569 Maple Street
Elm City, MI 90087
November 5, 1989

The Star-Times
27 River Street
Elm City, MI 90087

Dear Sir or Madam:

   I would like to apply for the job of Sunday carrier for your newspaper.

   I am thirteen years old, and a B+ student at Miller Junior High School. I have been a carrier for the Elm City Shopper for three years. I enjoy the work and think it is good experience because I would like to have a career in business some day. My supervisor at the Shopper is Mr. Alan Fisher, and I'm sure that he would give me a good reference. He can be reached at 988-7865.

   I would appreciate your giving me an interview, and would be glad to come at any time. My telephone number is 988-0987. Thank you.

Yours truly,

Name_____ Date_____

APPLYING FOR A JOB

DIRECTIONS: Write a letter of application for one of the following jobs. Be sure to state why you are interested, what qualifications you have for the job, and request an interview.

JOB 1: Cherokee Day Camp is looking for a junior counselor to help with their six-year-old campers. You must be at least thirteen years old, have experience with younger children, and be available for the month of July. They will provide transportation. Their address is 23 High Mountain Road, in your town.

JOB 2: The Times-Herald newspaper, located at 23 Broadway in your town, is looking for a carrier to deliver their daily newspaper daily between 4 and 5 P.M. They want someone who is good at figures since the carrier must collect money and keep records.

Write your letter here. Use correct business form.

_____

_____

_____

_____

_____

_____

_____

_____

_____

_____

_____

_____

_____

_____

_____

_____

_____

8

POETRY

Young students like poetry. They love the sound of rhythm and rhyme. They respond with enthusiasm to simple poems, are open to the nuances of metaphor and simile, can get excited about the sights and sounds of nature as captured in haiku, and can be persuaded to express their own thoughts and feelings with a minimum of motivation. They will even admit that they have fun doing it.

Somewhere around sixth or seventh grade things begin to change. Poetry gets to seem more and more esoteric, something that is as far removed from their own lives as a message in hieroglyphics. Perhaps this is because poetry has never been completely accepted as an art form by many people in this country. In some parts of the world, poetry is a highly admired means of expression, not just for graduate students and English majors, but for everyone. Common people, even those with little education, express themselves creatively by way of poetry and share their outpourings with one another without the slightest embarrassment. In our society, however, poets have been stereotyped as pale, fragile, ultrasensitive types.

By seventh grade, this negative attitude toward poetry is so strong that a teenager who likes to write poetry is already stigmatized as "different" or "intellectual." Junior or senior high school students, especially boys, who write poetry are apt to keep the fact to themselves. We need more poetry in our schools, not just the study of gifted poets of past and present, but hands-on experience to reacquaint students with the fun and fulfillment of poetic self-expression.

In recent years, a lot has been done along these lines by means of "poet in the classroom" projects and a proliferation of books and materials outlining methods of teaching poetry writing. Many of these programs and publications are wonderful, but most require much involvement on the part of the teacher and a genuine love of and commitment to poetry. The many excellent books available to guide the teacher of poetry include Kenneth Koch's *Wishes, Lies, and Dreams*, and *The Whole Word Catalogue*, which is put out by The Teachers and Writers Collaborative. These and others can be of immeasurable help to the teacher who is enthusiastic about poetry. This chapter, however, is designed for the average instructor who may or may not be a closet poet. Teacher participation is kept to a minimum. Most of the projects can be accomplished primarily through the use of Worksheets.

Activity 1   GETTING STARTED

We won't bring students into poetry by preaching about the eternal value of poetry, its universal appeal, its emphasis on capturing existence and creating truth through carefully selected words and phrases, rhythms, and, sometimes, rhyme. The aim of these activities is to demonstrate by hands-on participation the fun and excitement of poems. We want to sneak past any student prejudices by making a game out of poetry, and to begin with assignments that are simple enough for all to accomplish successfully.

This activity utilizes parallel poems. These are poems that use repetition. Each line begins with the same word or phrase, or contains some sort of repetition that appears in every line. Students find these easy to do and have fun with them. They can be used by students at all levels of ability. The writer can be merely superficial or can dig deeply into his or her imagination.

These beginning activities do not use rhyme. Not that students don't like rhyme. They love it—just listen to the songs they sing and the slogans they chant—but they don't do it well. It is extremely difficult to compose rhyme without ending up using words that are forced and phony, their only purpose being to achieve the rhyme. Try to convince the students that poetry need not be rhymed.

PREWRITING ACTIVITIES

1. Erase any inhibitions that may exist about poetry writing by creating a class poem. Ask each student to write one line beginning "I wish..." Then collect the papers and write all the lines on the chalkboard (or as many as you feel are necessary to get the idea across). Identify the result as a poem. Point out that it is not necessary for the lines to rhyme.

2. Create a second class parallel poem. Write the following lines on the chalkboard:
   I love the soft greens of spring
   And Halloween orange is the color of fun
Ask each student to write one line that contains a color. Then, have each student who is willing to do so copy his or her line onto the chalkboard. Read the resulting poem aloud.

3. Distribute Worksheet 8-1A I REMEMBER. Read the sample poem and the directions. (In regard to punctuation, suggest that the students use punctuation that shows phrasing and the end of a complete thought, as they would in prose. At this point, however, do not insist on correct punctuation or red-pencil incorrect punctuation on student poems. You want to encourage, not inhibit, free creative expression and a positive attitude toward poetry.)

4. When the students have completed their poems, divide into small groups and follow the process writing steps for critiquing and revising. Suggest that the critiquing groups look for interesting details that give insight into the writer's feelings and memories.

5. Distribute Worksheet 8-1B IF I WERE. Follow the same procedures as for worksheet 8-1A.

6. Distribute Worksheet 8-1C IN MY DREAMS. Follow the same procedures as for Worksheet 8-1A.

Activity 2   ACROSTIC POEMS

Like parallel poems, acrostic poems are easy and fun to write. Students usually enjoy doing them, partly because they like to work with their own names or with other words that have personal meaning to them, and partly because of the puzzle-solving aspects of this sort of writing. Some students actually become so obsessed with this activity that they spend their spare time working out poems based on the names of all their family members, friends, and even pets.

PREWRITING ACTIVITIES

1. You're going to have to introduce this activity by getting involved yourself. Write your own name on the chalkboard *vertically*. You can use your first name only, last name only, or your complete name. It will look like this:

M
A
R
Y
S
M
I
T
H

2. Tell the students that you are going to write a poem based on your name. Complete each of the lines you have begun on the chalkboard. (Of course, you will have prepared this in advance.) The poem should express something about you—your interests, appearance, activities, thoughts, etc.—as follows:

> My summers are always spent
> At a little cabin in the woods,
> Reading, hiking, fishing, and preparing
> Your lessons for the next
> School year; it is a
> Mystery to me how quickly the days go by.
> I love the warm sun glinting on the lake and
> The deep stillness of the forest; I laze about,
> Hoping it will never end.

3. Distribute Worksheet 8-2A ACROSTIC POEMS. Have the sample poems read aloud. Discuss these poems and elicit how they give some insight into the subject. Point out that these poems do not have to rhyme and that each line does not have to be a complete sentence. A thought may be continued on the next line if that fits the acrostic.

4. Distribute Worksheet 8-2B MY NAME. Read and discuss directions. When the students have completed their name poems, divide into small groups and follow process writing steps for critiquing and revising.

5. Distribute Worksheet 8-2C OTHER ACROSTICS. Read and discuss the samples in Part One.

6. Read the directions for Part Two. When the students have completed their poems, divide into small groups and follow process writing steps for critiquing and revising.

Activity 3   SENSE AND ACTION

The difference between flat, dry poetry and that which is evocative and experiential can be the judicious use of action and sensory language. Young writers should be encouraged to bring sensory imagery into their poetry and to create a feeling of action with strong verbs. The activities in this section will help your students acquire these valuable techniques.

PREWRITING ACTIVITIES

1. Write the following sets of lines on the chalkboard:

> the workman's hands
> the grey, gritty hands of the workman
>
> the beautiful sunset
> pinkish-purple sunset flush

> the clock on the tower tolled
> ding! dong! tolled the clock on the tower

Ask the students which lines create the most vivid impressions. Elicit the fact that the successful lines use sensory words.

2. Write the following lines on the chalkboard. (Leave space for a revised version beneath or alongside each line.)

> the school cafeteria
>
> a student stood up
>
> the pitcher threw the ball
>
> the nurse's smile

Brainstorm with the class and, together, come up with one or more revised versions of each line using sensory words and/or action to make a more vivid impression.

3. Distribute Worksheet 8-3A SENSE AND ACTION. Read and discuss the directions. When students have completed the activity, share and discuss the results. (This is not a draft, so do not use process writing steps for this activity.)

4. Distribute Worksheet 8-3B OTHER SENSES. Read and discuss the directions. Read and discuss the samples. Be sure the students understand that the goal of this activity is to combine and/or contrast several senses in one image. When the students have completed their poems, divide into small groups and follow process writing steps for critiquing and revising.

5. Distribute Worksheet 8-3C ACTION PLEASE. Read and discuss sample poems in Part One. Compare the two poems and have the students list the strong verbs that are used in Poem A.

6. Read and discuss the directions for Part Two. Be sure the students understand that the goal of this activity is to use strong, active verbs to create striking images. When the students have completed their poems, divide into small groups and follow process writing steps for critiquing and revising.

7. Distribute Worksheet 8-3D WHAT IS?. Read and discuss the directions. Read and discuss the samples and directions. Point out rhyme, but indicate that it may or may not be used. You may wish to omit critiquing and revising for these short poems, and just encourage class sharing.

8. Distribute Worksheet 8-3E HOW DOES IT SMELL?. Read and discuss the samples and directions. Again, you may wish to omit critiquing and revising and merely encourage class sharing.

Activity 4 FEELINGS AND RELATIONSHIPS

Poetry is a receptive medium for the expression of feelings. Creative expression has long been used as a catharsis for strong emotions. Feelings can be captured, condensed into words, and structured into a poem. No extended knowledge is required for such writing. Everyone knows what he or she feels or has felt on important or even not-so-special occasions. It takes only a small amount of direction and encouragement for students to pour these feelings into poetry.

Many of the strong emotions we experience arise out of relationships in our lives. Relationships with parents, with siblings, with teachers, with buddies, with classmates, with neighbors—all of these are accompanied by specific feelings. This activity, therefore, will include poems about relationships as well as feelings.

PREWRITING ACTIVITIES

1. Ask the students how many of them have ever felt extremely happy, terribly sad, deathly afraid, hugely embarrassed. Most of them will admit to these feelings. Choose one of these emotions, and write it on the chalkboard, such as:

FEAR

2. Ask the students to suggest words or phrases that this emotion evokes and list contributions on the chalkboard. It may look like this:

FEAR

   terrifying, ghastly, murder, shiver, pounding heart, legs trembling, shadows, nightmare, scream, horror, menacing, threatening, falling, drowning

3. Ask the class to compose together a short poem (two to four lines) about this emotion. Write it on the chalkboard.

4. Distribute Worksheet 8-4A FEELINGS. Read and discuss the directions. When the Worksheets have been completed, ask volunteers to share their lists with the class. The students can then add to their lists some of the words and phrases suggested by others.

5. Distribute Worksheet 8-4B MY FEELINGS. Read aloud the sample poem in Part A. Discuss the feelings that are represented. Ask the students to point out specific words and phrases that show these emotions.

6. Read and discuss the directions for Part Two. When the students have finished writing their poems, divide into groups and follow process writing steps for critiquing and revising.

7. Distribute Worksheet 8-4C FEELINGS AND PEOPLE. Read and discuss the directions for Part One. When the word lists in Part One have been completed, read and discuss the directions for Part Two. You may wish to omit group critiquing with this activity. Some students may be reluctant to share works that reveal their feelings about other people.

Activity 5   ANIMALS ——————————————————

Young people have a special affinity for animals. The old clichés about a kid and his or her dog or children at the zoo persist because they are true. Some children relate to pets better than they do to people. Often, they find it easier to let themselves go when writing about animals than with almost any other subject. Occasionally, a child will have a special interest in and knowledge about out-of-the-ordinary creatures, such as snakes or insects, or even an intense involvement with extinct species such as dinosaurs. Most students respond favorably to poetry activities involving animals.

PREWRITING ACTIVITIES

1. Read aloud to the class the following excerpt from a traditional American folk song.

   Rattlesnake, O rattlesnake,
   What makes your teeth so white?
   I've been in the bottom all my life,
   And I ain't done nothin' but bite, bite,
   Ain't done nothin' but bite.

   Muskrat, O muskrat,
   What makes you smell so bad?

I've been in the bottom all my life
Till I'm mortified in my head, head,
I'm mortified in my head.

2. Tell the class that they are going to compose a class poem that follows the same structure. Write the following lines on the chalkboard:

————, O ————,

What makes you ——————————?

I've ——————————————

————————————————————

————————————————————

3. Brainstorm with the class and encourage them to come up with appropriate words and phrases to fill in the blanks. (The first line will contain the creature's name twice; the second line will describe something it does or is; the third and fourth lines will describe the animal talking about its feelings; the last line will repeat part of the fourth.) Rhyme can be used as in the examples, but is not necessary.

4. Repeat this activity with another animal. If the class shows a lot of enthusiasm for this activity, the students can write individual poems about animals of their choice and then share them with the class. (Fourth-, fifth-, and sixth-graders will be more likely to want to do this than those in grades seven and eight.)

5. Distribute Worksheet 8-5A ANIMAL CRACKERS. Read and discuss the sample poems in Part One. Read and discuss the directions for Part Two. When the students have completed their poems, divide into groups and follow process writing steps for critiquing and revising.

6. Distribute Worksheet 8-5B INCREDIBLE BEASTS. Read and discuss the sample humorous animal poems in Part One. Read and discuss the directions for Part Two. When the students have completed their poems, divide into groups and follow process writing steps for critiquing and revising.

Activity 6   NATURE

Poetry and nature have always had a special relationship. Poets of the past and present have found inspiration in the wonders of the living Earth. Young people, too, can deepen their response to their natural surroundings by giving it form and structure in poetry.

PREWRITING ACTIVITIES

1. Read the following lines to the class:

Down in the valley, valley so low,
Hang your head over, hear the wind blow.
Hear the wind blow, dear, hear the wind blow,
Hang your head over, hear the wind blow.

Ask the students how many of them have ever heard the song, "Down in the Valley." Many, if not most, will respond affirmatively. Discuss the picture that is painted of someone looking down into a deep valley and listening to the sound of the wind. Point out that nature has always inspired strong feelings and that many people enjoy expressing these feelings in poems.

2. Distribute Worksheet 8-6A TREES AND BEES. Read and discuss the sample in Part One.

3. Read and discuss the directions for Part Two. When the students have completed their poems, divide into groups and follow process writing steps for critiquing and revising.

4. Distribute Worksheet 8-6B CABBAGE WINGS AND CATS ON MARS. Read and discuss the humorous poem in Part One.

5. Read and discuss the directions for Part Two. When the students have completed their poems, divide into groups and follow process writing steps for critiquing and revising.

6. Distribute Worksheet 8-6C HAIKU. Read and discuss Part One.

7. Read and discuss the directions for Part Two. When the students have completed their haiku poems, divide into groups and follow process writing steps for critiquing and revising.

Activity 7   USING RHYME

In the not-too-distant past, school children believed that all poetry rhymed. In fact, to them the word *poetry* meant just that—rhymed lines. When they attempted to write poetry themselves, this belief led to some charming verse, but also produced a lot of awkward, forced, often ridiculous rhymes.

In recent years, this trend has been reversed. Students are given a freer hand in shaping their attempts at poetry. No longer constrained by rhyming requirements, they can often turn out evocative, flowing word pictures that are genuine poetry.

Many times, rhyme is discouraged, or even disparaged. This is a shame because, while *good* rhyme is exceedingly difficult to accomplish successfully, the fact is that children (and many adults) really love the sound of rhyme. Look at the simple rhymes that are beloved from infancy on ("Twinkle, twinkle, little star; How I wonder what you are...") and the folk songs and verses that have captured the imaginations of ordinary people for generations ("Down in the valley, the valley so low; Hang your head over, hear the wind blow...").

While we want to avoid the trivialization of thought and image that often characterize student attempts at rhyme ("I love to feel the sun upon my skin; But first with suntan oil I must begin..."), we don't want them to miss the delighted response to language that rhyme can induce. In this section, students will find simple rhyming activities that are fun to do.

PREWRITING ACTIVITIES

1. Write the following on the chalkboard:

   I think that I shall never see
   A poem as lovely as a tree

Read these lines aloud. Tell the students they are from a poem called "Trees," by Joyce Kilmer. Ask the students what they notice about the last sound of each line. Elicit the fact that they rhyme. Ask for other words that rhyme with *see* and *tree*. Write these words on the chalkboard (*be, she, free,* etc.). Try to include a few words containing more than one syllable to demonstrate that the final sound is the one that must rhyme; e.g., *destiny, agree, dungaree,* etc.

2. Discuss the rhythm of these two lines. Tell the students that this verse contains a beat, like a song. Lead the class in saying the lines aloud, in unison. Emphasize the rhythm and the beat. Scan the syllables with the students and determine that there are eight syllables in each line. Elicit from the students that each beat contains two syllables, one soft and one stressed. Lead the class again in a unison recitation, emphasizing each strong beat. (da *dum*/da *dum*/da *dum*/ da *dum*). Ask the students how many beats are contained in each line (eight).

3. Tell the students that a pair of rhyming lines that contain the same number of beats is called a couplet. Write the word *couplet* on the chalkboard.

4. Write the following line on the chalkboard:

   I wish that I could be

   Lead the class in saying this line aloud. Elicit the number of beats (six). Suggest a possible second line, such as "Upon a ship at sea." Ask the students to supply an alternative second line that contains six beats and rhymes with the first. Write several of their suggestions on the chalkboard. Discuss how successful each one is in rhyming with the first and containing six beats.

5. Do this with several additional lines. You can make up your own, or use any of the following:

   In the morning, I arise (seven)
   The most exciting thing I know (eight)
   Tell me, have you ever seen (seven)

   Have the class read each line aloud and elicit the number of beats and the final sound that must be rhymed.

6. Distribute Worksheet 8-7A COUPLETS. Read the examples in Part One. Discuss rhyming sounds and number of beats.

7. Read the directions for Part Two. When students have completed their couplets, divide into groups and follow process writing steps for critiquing and revising. (Point out that critiquing should concentrate on rhythm and rhyme.)

8. Distribute Worksheet 8-7B ALPHABET SOUP. Read the first poem in Part One together. Instruct the students to write the letter *A* next to the first line, then to write the letter *A* next to any line that rhymes with the first. Tell them to write the letter *B* next to the second line, then to write *B* next to any line that rhymes with it. Ask them to read aloud the letters they have written in order (*ABAB*). Tell them that this describes the rhyme scheme. Follow the same procedures with the next poem. (The rhyme scheme will be *ABCB*.) Do the same with the last poem (*ABBA*).

9. Read the directions for Part Two. Be sure the students understand that they are to write two four-line poems, each with a different rhyme scheme. When the poems have been completed, divide into groups and follow process writing steps for critiquing and revising.

10. Distribute Worksheet 8-7C RHYME IN SONG. Read and discuss the examples in Part One. Read the directions for Part Two. When they have been completed, encourage students to share some of their song rhymes with the class. (Do not use process writing steps for this activity.)

Activity 8   LIMERICKS

Children enjoy limericks. They respond to the strong pattern of rhythm and rhyme. The intrinsic sense of silliness built into this verse form can be stimulating to a child's imagination and sense of humor.

At the beginning, some students may encounter difficulty recognizing and imitating the specific shape and pattern of limericks. The Worksheets in this activity are designed to bring students gradually and gently into a feeling for the form. By the time the last Worksheet has been completed, a student should be comfortable enough with the rhythm and rhyme pattern to be able to produce competently written limericks. The emphasis here should be on *fun*, so it would be best for you not to be rigid about complete accuracy in rhythm and rhyme. If the beat or the rhyme is off, don't make an issue of it. The preliminary Worksheets, however, should be a great help in training the student to write at least an approximation of the limerick.

PREWRITING ACTIVITIES

1. Recite a limerick to the class. Use one with which you are familiar, or the following:

   > There once was a lady from Niger
   > Who smiled as she rode on a tiger,
   > They returned from the ride
   > With the lady inside
   > And the smile on the face of the tiger.

   Elicit from the class that this verse form is called a limerick. Write the word *limerick* on the chalkboard.

2. Show the students that a limerick contains five lines. The first two and the last two are long. Lines three and four are short.

3. Elicit the rhyme scheme from the class. Ask a student to show this by writing the letters *A* and *B* after each line in the preceding example. It will look as follows:

   > A
   > A
   > B
   > B
   > A

4. Distribute Worksheet 8-8A LEARN THE LIMERICK. Have the class read aloud the example in Part One. Read and discuss the directions for analyzing the rhyme pattern and for filling in the blanks as they apply to the example.

5. Read and discuss the directions for Part Two. When the students have completed their fill-in limericks, encourage class sharing aloud. (Do not use process writing steps for this activity.)

6. Distribute Worksheet 8-8B FILL-IN LIMERICKS. Have the class read the example in Part One in unison.

7. Read and discuss the directions for Part Two. When the students have completed their fill-in limericks, encourage class sharing. (Do not use process writing steps for this activity.)

8. Distribute Worksheet 8-8C LIMERICK FUN. Read and discuss the directions. When the students have completed their limericks, divide into groups and follow process writing steps for critiquing and revising. (Direct groups to point out where their fellow students have strayed too far from the standard limerick pattern.)

Activity 9   GRAB BAG ────────────────────────────

This activity offers a grab bag of poetry-writing experiences that are interesting and challenging. Once students have been introduced to the creative, fun aspects of poetry, there are many kinds of poems with which they may wish to experiment. The Worksheets in this section will provide students with supplementary stimulating and creative activities, using various poetry and verse forms. Some of the forms explored are shape poems (concrete poetry), narrative poems, cinquain, and "me" poems.

These Worksheets are self-explanatory and can be used by students with or without teacher involvement, although fourth- and fifth-graders may benefit from some initial direction to be certain that they understand the requirements of the particular poetry form. At most, you may wish to provide motivation and guidance by going over the directions and, perhaps, sharing and discussing sample poems. Your participation and enthusiasm in this regard will certainly be of value, especially for younger students, but these Worksheets will work effectively on their own. Seventh- and eighth-graders, in particular, should be able to tackle them independently.

Do not omit the process writing steps for these Worksheets. Where there is less teacher direction, the benefits of peer critiquing, self-editing, and revising are even greater.

PREWRITING ACTIVITIES (FOR ALL WORKSHEETS IN THIS SECTION)

1. Distribute Worksheet.

2. (Optional) Read and discuss the sample poem and the particular poetry form used.

3. (Optional) Read and discuss the directions.

4. When students have completed their poems, divide into groups and follow process writing steps.

I REMEMBER

DIRECTIONS: There are many kinds of poems that are easy and fun to write. The poem below was written by a middle school student:

> I remember good times and bad times:
>
> I remember the day I had my tonsils out;
>
> I remember the bigness and whiteness of the hospital;
>
> I remember the hardness of the table;
>
> I remember waking up and my mom had ice cream for me.
>
> I remember the day I learned to ride a two-wheeler;
>
> I remember how Dad shoved the bike and ran after me;
>
> I remember how great I felt when he couldn't catch up.
>
> I remember shopping for school clothes last August;
>
> I remember my Mom saying I was driving her crazy.
>
> I remember the day I failed a math test;
>
> I remember wishing the ground would swallow me up.
>
> I remember my Grandpa Fred who died two years ago;
>
> I remember how he used to pat my head and give me a dollar.

This kind of poem is easy to write because every line begins with the same two words. Notice that the lines do not have to rhyme.

Write your own poem below. Begin each line with the words *I remember*. Make the poem as long as you wish, but try to have at least five lines.

_____

_____

_____

_____

_____

_____

_____

_____

_____

IF I WERE

DIRECTIONS: Here is a poem that is easy and fun to do. Note how the following lines all follow the same pattern.

> If I were an animal, I'd be an elephant in India.
>
> If I were a car, I'd be a red Porsche.
>
> If I were a city, I'd be Hollywood.
>
> If I were a river, I'd be the Nile in Egypt.
>
> If I were a pet, I'd be an independent cat.
>
> If I were a book, I'd be a romance novel.

How would you have completed these lines? Anyone can write this kind of poem, and then have additional fun by sharing the results with classmates. How are your classmates' poems different from yours? Do these poems give any insight into people? Complete the lines that are started for you below. Then, add any more that you can think of. You can choose from the list below for your extra lines, or come up with your own ideas.

a TV show	a flower
a piece of furniture	a machine
a newspaper or magazine	a school subject

IF I WERE

If I were an animal, I'd be _____

If I were a car, I'd be _____

If I were a city, I'd be _____

If I were a river, I'd be _____

If I were a pet, I'd be _____

If I were food, I'd be _____

If I were a planet, I'd be _____

If I were a board game, I'd be _____

If I were a building, I'd be _____

If I were a famous person, I'd be _____

If I were a sport, I'd be _____

_____

_____

Name_____ Date_____

IN MY DREAMS

DIRECTIONS: Here is a poem written by a seventh-grader.

> In my dreams,
> I am an important person.
> I wander through strange worlds,
> And sometimes fly above the clouds.
> In my dreams,
> I live in houses that are mazes.
> Monsters sometimes wait in shadows.
> In my dreams,
> I travel to far-off, silvery lands
> Where people and places appear, then melt away.

Write a poem about your dreams. You can begin each line with the same three words, "In my dreams…", or on some lines you can use connective words or commas to join the thoughts. Your dream images can be real or made up. Include at least five lines in your poem. It can be much longer, if you wish.

IN MY DREAMS

_____

_____

_____

_____

_____

_____

_____

_____

ACROSTIC POEMS

An acrostic poem is formed by writing a name or word vertically, and then creating a poem where each line begins with one letter of that name or word.

Notice that these poems do not have to rhyme. Also, you can begin a new line in the middle of a thought or sentence if that will fit the acrostic.

*M*itts and bats
*A*re my favorite sorts of equipment.
*T*hey are kept in a handy place so I can
*T*ake them each time I play
*O*n my Little League team; we're called the
*B*ears; we're the best team in the league—
*R*ight now we're in first place.
I know we'll win the championship
*E*asily because there's
*N*o other team that can beat us.

*S*ome day I'm going to be a famous
*A*ctress; I'll play all sorts of
*R*oles; sometimes I'll be
A good person and sometimes I'll be a
*D*evil; I'll play on TV, and
*O*n stage; I'll also
*B*e a star of the movies; I'll be
*I*n horror films and love stories, and
*E*verybody will want my autograph.

*R*unning is what I do best; I want to be
*O*n the track team in high school, and to
*B*e the fastest kid on the team.
*B*esides running
I'm also interested in
*E*very kind of animal; I like to
*R*ead about animals, and most of all
I love going to the zoo; I might become a
*V*et and take care of wild animals like
*E*lephants and
*R*hinos
And other creatures in the zoos.

MY NAME

DIRECTIONS: You are going to write an acrostic poem based on your own name.
   Write your name (first name, then last name) VERTICALLY on the lines below. Write one letter at the beginning of each line. It will look like this:

J
A
C
K
S
P
R
A
T

Each line of your poem will begin with one of the letters of your name. Your poem does not have to rhyme. You don't have to finish a thought or sentence on a line. You can continue it on a new line if that fits the acrostic. The poem should be about you. (Read the sample acrostic poems on Worksheet 8-2A to see how it's done.)

MY NAME POEM

_____

_____

_____

_____

_____

_____

_____

_____

_____

_____

_____

_____

_____

_____

_____

Name_____ Date_____

OTHER ACROSTICS

PART ONE: You can write an acrostic poem about anything—friends' names, pets, other animals, objects, etc. Here are acrostics that some students have written:

Devoted to
One master,
Grand, loving pet.

Baseball is the game I play
And love; every day after
School, I meet the
Eight other guys on my
Ball team; we practice
And play and work hard to
Learn the game so we will
Lead the League.

The big cat
Is fast and smart,
Growl is a warning to
Every other creature to
Run away quickly.

Shining above, around,
Under our Earth,
Nothing exists,
Nothing lives without
You.

PART TWO: Choose a name or object or word and write it vertically, one letter at the beginning of each line, as in the samples above. Then, complete your poem. Write as many acrostic poems as you can. Use the back of this paper if you need more room.

ACROSTIC POEMS

_____

_____

_____

_____

_____

_____

_____

_____

_____

_____

_____

_____

SENSE AND ACTION

DIRECTIONS: Anyone can produce poetry that is delightful to read and fun to write. One way that usually works is to try to use as many sensory words and strong, active verbs as possible.

Words that show smell, sight, taste, touch, and sound help you to "paint with words" and create images that are vivid and exciting. The same is true of strong action verbs, such as *devour* or *gnaw* instead of *eat*, and *stumble* or *stroll* instead of *walk*.

The lines below are flat and dull. Can you make them more interesting by using sensory words and strong action verbs? Write your revised line under each dull one. (Hint: Colors are sensory words that can accomplish a lot.)

1. The girl was on the beach.

   _____

2. She wore a hat.

   _____

3. The waves were loud.

   _____

4. She felt sand on her feet.

   _____

5. Two boys were in the water.

   _____

6. They played with a ball.

   _____

7. A child at water's edge.

   _____

8. Was making a fort.

   _____

OTHER SENSES

DIRECTIONS: Words that appeal to the senses help bring poetry to life. Painters mix colors on a palette to create a more beautiful picture than they could make using only one color. In the same way, a combination of sensory words can be used to paint a more effective "word picture" in poetry. How many senses are included in this poem?

Deep green is soft
Like thick, plush carpeting.
Light green sprays a fresh scent
Like air after a spring rain.
Faded green tastes sour
Like deli pickles.
And on my aunt's couch
Large green flowers race across the cushions
Like a scream in the morning.

If you counted five senses in this poem, you are right. The different *greens* for *sight; soft, thick, plush* refers to the sense of *touch; fresh, scent,* and *air* indicate *smell; sour* and *deli pickles* bring *taste* to mind; and *scream* is for *sound.*

You are going to write a poem below. Try to use words and phrases that bring into play more than one sense. You don't have to include all the senses as in the example above, but use *at least* two senses in your poem. It's fun and a challenge to use as many senses as possible.

Write a color poem, like the one above. Color poems are easy to compose because colors can bring so many different things to our minds. If you have trouble getting started, begin with "Blue is..." or "Bright yellow..."

_____

_____

_____

_____

_____

_____

_____

_____

_____

_____

ACTION PLEASE!

PART ONE: Compare poems A and B.

A	B
In my dream	In my dream
I walk on the beach,	I trudge along the beach,
My feet in the sand.	My feet sinking into the sand.
I see a huge wave	I gape at a huge wave
Coming toward shore.	Galloping toward the shore.
I try to move my feet,	I try to wrench my feet loose,
But they are going down,	But they are sucked down, down,
And the wave comes at me.	And the wave roars toward me.

The action in Poem B is more exciting because of the strong verbs. On the line below, list some of the powerful action words that make this poem more interesting.

_____

PART TWO: Write a poem describing a dream or any other scene that you can see clearly in your mind. You might want to write about an exciting moment in a basketball game, or someone trying to escape from danger, or a thrilling ride in an amusement park. Make your poem vivid by using strong action words.

_____

_____

_____

_____

_____

_____

_____

_____

_____

_____

_____

WHAT IS?

Sometimes, it is fun to write poems based on just one sense, such as these:

What is white?	What is brown?
Clouds are white	Leaves are brown
Floating out of sight.	As they sail on down.
What is gold?	What is pink?
A crown is gold	A rose is pink
On a queen of old.	Lifting its satin face.

What sense do these poems describe? If you said *sight*, you are correct. What's more, they all refer to color. The same kind of poems can be written about other senses as well. They are easy to write. The first line asks the question. The second line answers the question. The third line extends the description.

In some of the sample poems, the third line rhymes with the first two. In which poem does the third line not rhyme? If you said the last, you are correct. Your own poems can rhyme or not—that is up to you.

Write four three-line poems below. They are all started for you.

What is blue?_____

_____

_____

What is bitter?_____

_____

_____

What is loud?_____

_____

_____

What is bumpy?_____

_____

_____

Name_____ Date_____

WHAT DOES IT SMELL LIKE?

What did the writer do in the poems below?

> The wind tastes like a fizzy coke.
>
> The wind smells like flower petals.
>
> The wind looks like a witch's hair.
>
> The wind sounds like a drum roll.
>
> The wind feels like rushing water.
>
> Daisies smell like expensive perfume.
>
> Daisies look like pats of butter.
>
> Daisies feel like yellow velvet.
>
> Daisies sound like whispering breezes.
>
> Daisies taste like sunshine.

All five senses are used in these poems to describe one word. Each line paints a word picture with one sense. In the same way, finish each of the poems below.

An apple smells _____

An apple tastes _____

An apple sounds _____

An apple looks _____

An apple feels _____

Pine trees smell_____

Pine trees feel _____

Pine trees look_____

Pine trees sound_____

Pine trees taste_____

Choose your own topic for the poem below. Begin each line with the subject's name; then finish each line with a different sense image.

_____

_____

_____

_____

FEELINGS

Everyone has feelings. Sometimes, we may be especially happy. Other times, we are sad. There are moments when we are afraid or ashamed. Other times, we may feel brave and daring. It's fun to write about our feelings. Our writing will be more successful if we know a lot of words and phrases that can describe our feelings.

In the boxes below, write as many words and phrases you can think of that can have something to do with the feeling listed at the top of the box.

HAPPINESS

SADNESS

ANGER

FEAR

LOVE

HATE

MY FEELINGS

PART ONE: Read the poem below.

> Like one, that on a lonesome road
> Doth walk in fear and dread,
> And having once turned round walks on,
> And turns no more his head;
> Because he knows a frightful fiend
> Doth close behind him tread.
> (from "The Rime of the Ancient Mariner"
> by Samuel Taylor Coleridge)

What feeling does this poem show?⎯⎯⎯⎯⎯⎯⎯⎯⎯⎯⎯⎯⎯⎯⎯⎯⎯⎯⎯⎯⎯

List the words and phrases that indicate this feeling.⎯⎯⎯⎯⎯⎯⎯⎯⎯⎯⎯⎯⎯⎯

⎯⎯⎯⎯⎯⎯⎯⎯⎯⎯⎯⎯⎯⎯⎯⎯⎯⎯⎯⎯⎯⎯⎯⎯⎯⎯⎯⎯⎯⎯⎯⎯⎯⎯

PART TWO: Think about a time when you had a strong feeling about something (love, hate, fear, happiness, sadness, or anger). Write a poem about it below. (Consult Worksheet 8-4A for words and phrases that you might use.)

⎯⎯⎯⎯⎯⎯⎯⎯⎯⎯⎯⎯⎯⎯⎯⎯⎯⎯⎯⎯⎯⎯⎯⎯⎯⎯⎯⎯⎯⎯⎯⎯⎯⎯

⎯⎯⎯⎯⎯⎯⎯⎯⎯⎯⎯⎯⎯⎯⎯⎯⎯⎯⎯⎯⎯⎯⎯⎯⎯⎯⎯⎯⎯⎯⎯⎯⎯⎯

⎯⎯⎯⎯⎯⎯⎯⎯⎯⎯⎯⎯⎯⎯⎯⎯⎯⎯⎯⎯⎯⎯⎯⎯⎯⎯⎯⎯⎯⎯⎯⎯⎯⎯

⎯⎯⎯⎯⎯⎯⎯⎯⎯⎯⎯⎯⎯⎯⎯⎯⎯⎯⎯⎯⎯⎯⎯⎯⎯⎯⎯⎯⎯⎯⎯⎯⎯⎯

⎯⎯⎯⎯⎯⎯⎯⎯⎯⎯⎯⎯⎯⎯⎯⎯⎯⎯⎯⎯⎯⎯⎯⎯⎯⎯⎯⎯⎯⎯⎯⎯⎯⎯

⎯⎯⎯⎯⎯⎯⎯⎯⎯⎯⎯⎯⎯⎯⎯⎯⎯⎯⎯⎯⎯⎯⎯⎯⎯⎯⎯⎯⎯⎯⎯⎯⎯⎯

⎯⎯⎯⎯⎯⎯⎯⎯⎯⎯⎯⎯⎯⎯⎯⎯⎯⎯⎯⎯⎯⎯⎯⎯⎯⎯⎯⎯⎯⎯⎯⎯⎯⎯

⎯⎯⎯⎯⎯⎯⎯⎯⎯⎯⎯⎯⎯⎯⎯⎯⎯⎯⎯⎯⎯⎯⎯⎯⎯⎯⎯⎯⎯⎯⎯⎯⎯⎯

⎯⎯⎯⎯⎯⎯⎯⎯⎯⎯⎯⎯⎯⎯⎯⎯⎯⎯⎯⎯⎯⎯⎯⎯⎯⎯⎯⎯⎯⎯⎯⎯⎯⎯

⎯⎯⎯⎯⎯⎯⎯⎯⎯⎯⎯⎯⎯⎯⎯⎯⎯⎯⎯⎯⎯⎯⎯⎯⎯⎯⎯⎯⎯⎯⎯⎯⎯⎯

FEELINGS AND PEOPLE

PART ONE: We usually have lots of feelings about people. Some of these feelings may be pleasant. Others may not be so pleasant. Some may even be funny. You're going to write about someone you know and your feelings about this person. First, you're going to get ready by making some lists. In each of the boxes below, write as many words and phrases you can think of that have something to do with your feelings about the person named in the box.

MY MOTHER (OR FATHER)

A BROTHER, SISTER, OR OTHER RELATIVE

ONE OF MY FRIENDS OR CLASSMATES

Choose one of the people above, and write a poem describing how you feel about that person. (You will not have to share this poem if you prefer not to.)

_____

_____

_____

_____

_____

_____

Name_____ Date_____

ANIMAL CRACKERS

PART ONE: Read the two poems below. The first was written by a famous poet. The other is by a seventh-grade student.

THE TIGER
Tyger! Tyger! burning bright
In the forests of the night.
What immortal hand or eye
Could frame thy fearful symmetry?
—William Blake

THIS KITTEN
This kitten is like a ball of fur,
Bouncing across the room
Chasing his tail round and round
Like a cottony top;
This kitten leaps into my lap,
Twitching his small pointed ears,
and purrs softly like a luxury car;
This kitten loves me.

One of the animals described is wild; the other is a pet. In each case, the reader can almost see the creature. Some of the words that help are *burning bright, forests of the night, ball of fur, bouncing, twitching, purrs softly,* etc.

PART TWO: On the lines below, write your own poem about an animal. Choose something that you really like and can picture in your mind's eye. Use any form you wish for your poem. Use sensory words and action to paint a word picture.

_____

_____

_____

_____

_____

_____

_____

_____

_____

_____

_____

_____

INCREDIBLE BEASTS

PART ONE: Are real animals described in the following poems?

EARWIG
The horny goloch is an awesome beast,
Supple and scaly;
It has two horns, and a hantle of feet,
And a forkie tailie.
                    —Traditional Scottish song

THE MARZIPLE
The marziple has tiny pointed ears
And three round orange eyes
And a slimy green shell.
It slithered down to Earth one day
And landed in my bed,
YUCK!
                —by a sixth-grade student

MY INCREDIBLE BEAST

Have you ever seen a three-eyed marziple slithering down to Earth or a horny goloch with its forkie tailie? Of course not! They are fantastic creatures from the writer's imagination.

PART TWO: Write a poem about an incredible beast. You can make the creature as unbelievable, scary, horrible, disgusting, or funny as you wish. You can show it doing ridiculous, frightening, or humorous things. You can even use made-up words. First, think of a name for your incredible beast. Write the name as a title on the first line, and write your poem below. You may also draw it above, if you wish.

_____

_____

_____

_____

_____

_____

_____

_____

_____

_____

_____

_____

_____

TREES AND BEES

PART ONE: The following poem was written more than a hundred years ago by Thomas Moore.

> I have a garden of my own,
>   Shining with flowers of every hue;
> I loved it dearly while alone,
>   But I shall love it more with you;
> And there the golden bees shall come,
>   In summer time at break of morn,
> And wake us with their busy hum
>   Around the fragrant thorn.

Can you picture the garden with its flowers and bees? The poet may have been in the garden when he wrote this, or he may have been remembering it, or it might just have been a picture in his imagination. What do you think?

PART TWO: It's fun to write poems about nature. Try to recall an outdoor spot that you have seen recently. It could be a garden, or an oceanside beach or a grassy lawn or a tree-lined street where you have walked. You could look out the classroom window and describe what you see there. Here are some other scenes you might like to write about: a sparrow on a tree branch, ducks in a pond, a lake in the rain, falling leaves, a snow scene. Think about the scene for a while. Try to recall what you saw there, the colors, the movements, the shapes. How did it make you feel? Write a poem below about this scene. Try to use sensory and action words to make the spot come alive.

_____

_____

_____

_____

_____

_____

_____

_____

_____

_____

_____

_____

_____

CABBAGE WINGS AND CATS ON MARS

PART ONE: Poems about nature don't have to be serious. It can be fun to describe a scene humorously, as in the poem below:

> ### THE VEGGIE BIRD
> The veggie bird has cabbage wings
> And nibbles corn seed as it flies.
> Its orange carrot nose is bright,
> Its avocado beak's a sight,
> And tiny green peas serve as eyes.
> The birdlings live in broccoli nests;
> Of all birds, they're the healthiest.
> So if you eat your veggies, you
> Can be a strong veggie bird, too.

PART TWO: Can you write a humorous poem about nature? You can choose one of the subjects listed on Worksheet 8-6A or make up one of your own. Here are some additional suggestions: a dog swimming across a lake, frogs crossing a snowpile, a bee that can't find flowers, a black cloud that can't produce rain, an upside-down garden, a jungle filled with odd flowers and creatures, an unhappy flower, a cat on Mars.

Write the name of your poem on the first line.

——

——

——

——

——

——

——

——

——

——

HAIKU

PART ONE: The Japanese people have been writing tiny poems about nature for hundreds of years. These are called *haiku*. In Japan, ordinary people, young and old, in all walks of life, love to write haiku. In recent years, they have become popular in this country, too. They are so easy to write, and fun as well.

The rules are simple. Haiku has three lines and seventeen syllables, divided as follows:

• The first line has five syllables.

• The second line has seven syllables.

• The third line has five syllables.

Most haiku will mention the name of a season or show, in some way, which season is being described. Here are some examples.

Cruel autumn wind	Mountain-rose petals
Cutting to the very bones	Falling, falling, falling now
Of my poor scarecrow.	Waterfall music.
Mirror-pond of stars;	This snowy morning
Suddenly a summer shower	The black crow I hate so much,
Dimples the water.	But he's beautiful!

Say each of these haiku aloud. Count the syllables as you say them. Can you hear the pattern for each line: five, seven, five?

PART TWO: When you write your own haiku, it will be easy if you keep it simple. Stick to one small subject for each poem. Use strong sensory and action words. The first three haiku are begun for you. You just have to add lines two (seven syllables) and three (five syllables). After that, write one (or more) three-line haiku of your own.

1

Winter freezes trees

_____

_____

2

A spring bud opens

_____

_____

3

Summer ocean waves

_____

_____

4

_____

_____

_____

5

_____

_____

_____

6

_____

_____

_____

Name_____ Date_____

COUPLETS

PART ONE: Two-line verses that rhyme are called *rhymed couplets*.

1	2
Twinkle, twinkle, little star—	Oh do you know old Mr. Fell?
How I wonder what you are	Indeed I know him very well.
3	**4**
The bird sang in the tree	Many days have passed since then
It sang tooroo, tooree	I never will go back again
5	**6**
My country 'tis of thee	Once upon a midnight dreary
Sweet land of liberty	As I pondered weak and weary

Read each couplet aloud. Show below the rhyming words and number of beats for each. (The first one is done for you.)

1. Rhyming Words: __star, are__; Number of beats: __7__

2. Rhyming Words: _____; Number of beats: ____

3. Rhyming Words: _____; Number of beats: ____

4. Rhyming Words: _____; Number of beats: ____

5. Rhyming Words: _____; Number of beats: ____

6. Rhyming Words: _____; Number of beats: ____

PART TWO: Rhymed couplets are easy and fun to do. They can be serious or humorous. Write as many rhymed couplets as you can in the time allotted by your teacher. The first four are begun for you.

1. I wish I could be

_____

3. The kitty loves to play

_____

5. _____

_____

7. _____

_____

9. _____

_____

2. I sometimes walk out in the snow

_____

4. Birds are singing in the trees

_____

6. _____

_____

8. _____

_____

10. _____

_____

ALPHABET SOUP

PART ONE: There are many different kinds of rhymes. Here's one.

1. **When icicles hang by the wall,**
   And Dick the shepherd blows his nail,
   And Tom bears logs into the hall,
   And milk comes frozen home in pail.
   —William Shakespeare

Here's how you can figure out the rhyme plan for this poem. First, write the letter *A* after the first line. Write another *A* next to the line that rhymes with it. Then, write the letter *B* after the second line. Write *B* at the end of another line that rhymes with this one. If you did it correctly, it will look like this:

When icicles hang by the wall,	A
And Dick the shepherd blows his nail,	B
And Tom bears logs into the hall,	A
And milk comes frozen home in pail.	B

This rhyme plan is called *ABAB*. Do the same for the next poems. (A line that doesn't rhyme with either the first or second line will be labeled *C*.) When you have finished writing the rhyme schemes, compare your results with the answers at the bottom of this Worksheet.

2. **The Sun came up upon the left,**
   Out of the sea came he!
   And he shone bright, and on the right
   Went down into the sea.
   —Samuel T. Coleridge

3. **The winter's long and cold and grey**
   And seems to have no end,
   But waiting round the bend
   Is spring in all its bright array.

PART TWO: Write two original four-line poems. Use a different rhyme scheme for each.

1. _____

_____

_____

_____

2. _____

_____

_____

_____

(Rhyme scheme for poem 2 is *ABCB*; for 3—*ABBA*.)

Name _____ Date _____

RHYME IN SONG

PART ONE: Poetry is a lot like song. They both have rhythm and they both often have rhyme. What are the rhyme schemes in the song lyrics below? (Write the letters *A, B, C*, etc. at the end of each line.)

1. Twinkle, twinkle, little star,
   How I wonder what you are,
   Up above the world so high
   Like a diamond in the sky.

2. Jingle bells, jingle bells,
   Jingle all the way,
   Oh, what fun it is to ride
   In a one-horse open sleigh.

3. Down in the valley,
   Valley so low,
   Hang your head over,
   Hear the wind blow.

4. Old King Cole was a merry old soul,
   And a merry old soul was he,
   He called for his pipe and he called for his bowl,
   And he called for his fiddlers three.

The correct rhyme schemes for these songs are: 1. *AABB*; 2. *ABCB*; 3. *ABCB*; 4. *ABAB*.

PART TWO: On the lines below, write the lyrics to a song that you know or one that you have made up yourself. At the bottom, write the rhyme scheme for this song, using *A, B, C*, etc.

_____

_____

_____

_____

_____

_____

_____

_____

_____

_____

_____

(Write the rhyme scheme here:) _____

LEARN THE LIMERICK

PART ONE: Read the following limerick aloud.

> There was an old man from Peru
> Who dreamt he was eating his shoe,
> He awoke in the night
> In a terrible fright
> To find that his dream had come true!
>   —Edward Lear

Show the rhyme pattern of this limerick. Write the letter *A* next to the first line and put an *A* next to every other line that rhymes with it. Write the letter *B* next to the third line and put a *B* next to any line that rhymes with it.

If you wrote *AABBA*, you are correct. A limerick consists of five lines. Lines one, two, and five have one rhyme. Lines three and four have another.

Look at the length of each line. You will notice that lines one, two, and five are long. Lines three and four are short. The dashes below show the pattern of the limerick. Copy this limerick below, putting one syllable (beat) on each dash.

_____ _____ _____ _____ _____ _____ _____ _____

_____ _____ _____ _____ _____ _____ _____ _____

_____ _____ _____ _____ _____ _____

_____ _____ _____ _____ _____ _____

_____ _____ _____ _____ _____ _____ _____ _____

PART TWO: The limerick below is only partly written. Complete it by filling in the blanks with your own words. You can be as silly as you like. Be sure you follow the rhyme scheme as in Part One.

There was a _____ boy in a store

Who said, "I won't _____ _____ more,"

His _____ replied

"_____ _____ outside

And don't _____ _____ _____ _____ _____" (must rhyme with *store*)

Name_____   Date_____

FILL-IN LIMERICKS

PART ONE: Read the following limerick aloud, noting the rhythm and rhyme plan.

> There was an old man of Berlin
> Whose form was uncommonly thin;
> Till he once, by mistake,
> Was mixed up in a cake,
> So they baked that Old Man of Berlin.
> —Edward Lear

PART TWO: The limericks below are only partially written. Complete them by filling in the blanks with your own words. Remember that lines one, two, and five rhyme with each other; lines three and four rhyme.

1. There was a _____ _____ from the East

   Who once _____ _____ _____ _____ beast

   The _____ creature cried

   _____ _____ _____ _____ (must rhyme with *cried*)

   And _____ _____ _____ _____ _____ _____ (rhyme with *East*)

2. There was a _____ _____ from Salt Lake

   Who _____ _____ _____ _____ chocolate cake,

   One day _____ _____ _____   (These two lines

   _____ _____ _____ _____ _____   must rhyme.)

   And now _____ _____ _____ _____ _____ _____ (rhyme with *cake*)

3. There was a _____ _____ named LeRoy

   Who wanted _____ _____ _____ _____ _____ (rhyme with *LeRoy*)

   He went to _____ _____   (These two lines

   And _____ _____ _____ _____   must rhyme.)

   And now he _____ _____ _____ _____ _____. (rhyme with *LeRoy*)

LIMERICK FUN

DIRECTIONS: It's fun to make up humorous limericks. Here's a silly one:

> There was an Old Man with a beard
> Who said, "It is just as I feared!
> Two owls and a Hen,
> Four larks and a Wren,
> Have all built their nests in my beard."
> —Edward Lear

A limerick contains five lines. Lines one, two, and five are longer and rhyme with each other. Lines three and four are short and rhyme. Can you write some five-line limericks? They can be as silly and ridiculous as you wish. Here are some suggestions for first lines, or you can use your own:

There once was a goose with two heads
There was a boy who loved TV
There was a bear living in town
There was a tall girl in New York
There was a peacock in the zoo
There once was a mouse on a chair
There once was a fat kangaroo
There once was a horse who ate oats

Write your limericks on the lines below. Use the back of this Worksheet if you need more room.

1. _____

_____

_____

_____

2. _____

_____

_____

_____

Name_____   Date_____

SHAPE POEMS

PART ONE: Here are some unusual poems.

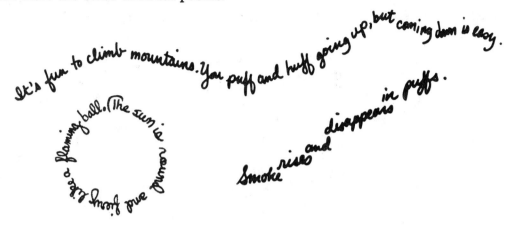

These are called shape (or concrete) poems because they combine words and space to create a picture or shape. Notice how the poem about mountains is written as a hilly outline, the sun poem forms a circle, and the poem about smoke looks like smoke rising into the air.

PART TWO: Follow the instructions below for creating your own shape poems.

1. Write a poem about something that is circular in shape, such as wheels, a doorknob, a globe, the moon, a birthday cake, a balloon, someone's head, or any other circular object you can think of. Write your poem around the circle below.

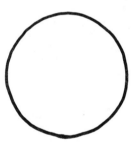

2. Write a poem about something that is rectangular in shape, such as a box, a book, a football field, a bed, a pillow, a table, or any other rectangle.

3. Can you think of any other shape poems? Write them on the back of this Worksheet.

NARRATIVE POEMS

PART ONE: A poem that tells a story is a narrative poem. You've probably read some familiar ones such as "The Owl and the Pussycat" or "Hiawatha." Here is another such poem.

BONNIE GEORGE CAMPBELL

High upon the Highlands
   And low upon Tay,
Bonnie George Campbell,
   Rode out on a day.
He saddled, he bridled,
   And gallant rode he,
And home came his good horse,
   But never came he.
Out came his mother dear,
   Wild with despair;
And out came his bonnie bride,
   Tearing her hair.
"My meadow lies green
   And my corn is unshorn,
My barn is unbuilt,
   And my babe is unborn."
Saddled and bridled
   And booted rode he,
A plume in his helmet,
   A sword at his knee.
Safe home came his saddle,
   All bloody to see,
Oh, home came his good horse,
   But never came he.

This poem tells a mysterious story about a horse that came home without its rider. Not all story-poems are exciting. Some are humorous or just pleasant to read.

PART TWO: Write your own narrative poem below. It can rhyme or not. You can write an exciting story-poem about knights and dragons, or space adventures or even a gory accident. Or, write a humorous story-poem about silly humans or animals, or one about your own typical day. Just tell a story in poem form. Write your rough draft below.

_____

_____

_____

_____

_____

_____

_____

(Continue your narrative poem on the back of this Worksheet.)

(8-9B)

CINQUAIN

PART ONE: The cinquain is a poem where the syllables are counted (like haiku). The cinquain has five lines. The first line has two syllables; the second line has four syllables; the third line has six syllables; the fourth line has eight syllables; the fifth line has two syllables.

DAWN
_____ I wept
_____ As the blossoms
_____ Opened in the morning
_____ Mist; dew slid down the petals like
_____ My tears.

In the above poem, count the number of syllables in each line. Write the total in the blank. If you count correctly, your numbers will look like this:

2
4
6
8
2

PART TWO: It's fun to write cinquains. They can be about anything, even something you can see around you now—perhaps someone's head bent over the desk, her long hair spilling over the paper, or the wide, friendly smile that kid at the end of the third row always has on his face. Or, look out the window and observe a bird or trees or people rushing along the sidewalk. Or, it can be some memory you have. Just be sure to use five lines and count the syllables as above. Write at least two cinquains, more if you like. (Use the back of this Worksheet if you need more room.)

1. _____

_____

_____

_____

_____

2. _____

_____

_____

_____

_____

"ME" POEMS

PART ONE: There is one person who is more interesting than anyone else in the world. That is your own self. Everyone thinks about himself or herself a lot. We're always learning something about ourselves whether we are changing and growing or staying the same. We think about things we do well, ways in which we wish we were different, embarrassing moments, happy times, how we relate to other people and to the world around us. It's fun to put these thoughts and feelings into poems. Here are some examples of "me" poems.

1	**2**
My heart leaps up when I behold	I am a tiny worm
A rainbow in the sky	An invisible germ,
So was it when my life began;	Like a fly on a wall,
So is it now I am a man;	No one seems to
So be it when I shall grow old.	See me at all.
Or, let me die!	

—William Wordsworth

Poem 1 was written by a famous poet in a happy mood. Poem 2 was written by a seventh-grade student who was feeling down. They are both good "me" poems because they tell something about the writer and his or her thoughts or feelings.

PART TWO: "Me" poems are easy to write. If you're feeling great, writing about how lovely things are can make you feel even more super. If you're feeling sad, giving shape to your feelings in a poem can make you feel better. Try it! Write at least two "me" poems below.

_____

_____

_____

_____

_____

_____

_____

_____

_____

_____

_____

_____

(Use the back of this Worksheet if you need more room.)

9

PUBLICATION

There is nothing that sparks a student's desire to write effectively as much as the possibility of publication. The prospect of seeing one's work in print is the most effective motivational device that is available to the teacher of writing. Publication lends an importance to writing that cannot be approached by mere classroom assignments or even grades. Even professional authors admit that the prospect of fame and fortune is an incentive that inspires labor. "No man but a blockhead," said Samuel Johnson, "ever wrote, except for money." For the student-writer, publication is an effective substitute.

There are many more possibilities for student publication than is generally realized. These range from a modest, mimeographed two-page collection of verse for the students to take home after a poetry unit all the way to submission of student work to national publications that actually offer payment for accepted pieces. This chapter suggests how to realize these possibilities.

GENERAL STRATEGIES

You must determine which type of publication effort best suits the students' particular needs and goals. Some of the factors you will wish to consider are:

1. What is the scope and purpose of your publishing requirements? Are you trying to encourage talented writers to seek regional or national publication? Do you want an in-class project where all writers of any ability can see their work in print? Are you looking for effective display material for a school open house for parents and/or community? Would a writing project for a single grade suit your needs? Do you want an all-school writing publication? Do you want your publishing venture to be part of a city, regional, or state writing program? Or would you like some combination of two or more of the foregoing? It is important that you decide on the preferred scope of your publishing venture before checking the other factors.

2. How will your school policies and restrictions affect your decision? Are interdisciplinary activities encouraged? Will there be a problem putting into effect a project that may require the cooperation of all the teachers in a grade or even the entire school?

3. How will this fit into your curriculum? Would an in-class publication best meet your curriculum goals? Would the activities involved in producing a school publication have any effect on your course of study? Would there be a place for efforts to submit work to outside publications?

4. What is your financial situation? The simplest in-class project involves nothing more than paper and access to a copying machine. Are funds available for a more ambitious class or grade-level publication? A school newspaper or school literary magazine can be a lot more expensive, especially if a professional printing job is desired. Participation in district or regional writing workshops will also require extra funding. Will this be available?

5. What time requirements are involved? Will the work be done during or after school hours? If after school, do you have a committed staff? Is this a one-shot deal or a continuing project?

Once you have decided on the type of publication effort that is right for your purposes, consult the appropriate activity (or activities) that follow for guidance and suggestions.

Activity 1   IN-CLASS PUBLICATIONS

There are several ways that you can compile the writing efforts of your class in a form that will give the students the satisfaction of feeling "published." You can prepare an anthology of student work after a particular unit (i.e., poetry or fiction writing or writing geared to a particular holiday or season), and make a copy for each student in the class. You can compile a larger, more varied anthology at the end of a semester. You can publish an in-class newspaper that appears monthly, bi-monthly, or several times a year. Your students can write and illustrate individual "books" that can be put together easily and inexpensively. The directions and Worksheets in this activity will help you put together an in-class publication.

SPECIAL ANTHOLOGY (to follow a particular writing unit)

1. Be sure all the students have gone through all steps of the process writing method and have available the final, best copy of their work.

2. For the easiest and quickest anthology, just make copies of each student's handwritten work (this can include illustrations as well as writing), staple the pages together, and distribute. This will give the students a chance to read the efforts of their classmates, and (if the booklet makes it back home) give the same opportunity to their parents. The project can be made even more attractive, with a minimum of effort, by including a cover page containing the school name, class, date, teacher's name and, perhaps, a catchy title for the project. Teacher or student illustrations can adorn the cover, if desired. The cover page might look like this:

3. The students will have a greater feeling of being published if a slightly more professional-looking booklet is produced, one that is typed or word processed. This will involve collecting student work and typing it in neatly arranged pages. You will have to do the typing yourself unless you can find a parent volunteer or have clerical assistance available in the school office. Another possibility is to work out an interdisciplinary effort if there is a typing class in your school. Older students with typing skills might be willing to do this at home or in school. The cover page, too, can be typed, giving the whole project a more professional look. Doing the cover on colored stock is a nice touch. If you have access to a computer and dot matrix or laser printer, you can design an impressive-looking booklet. If this is the culmination of a special unit (for example, a Haiku pamphlet), it won't be as much work as it sounds since a lot of handwritten material will usually fit on one typewritten page, and only a few pages will probably be involved.

END OF SEMESTER "BEST OF ..." ANTHOLOGY

1. This format can be used at the end of a semester or school year, and will contain a selection of the best of your students' writing. The anthology may contain examples of various kinds of writing, including poetry, fiction, and essays, or your class can produce several anthologies—one for poetry, another for fiction, etc.

2. The first step is to determine the criteria for content selection, and who should make these choices. Each child in the class should be represented by at least one selection. Beyond that, the most outstanding work can be chosen either by you or by a committee of students. The committee should be small—no more than two or three students (otherwise cliques and bickering may develop). This editorial committee can be elected by the class or appointed by you. An appointed committee usually works best since one that is elected may become just a popularity contest, while you can select students whom you believe to be insightful and responsible.

2. If the anthology is a general one, there should be adequate representation among the various genres such as poetry, fiction, etc. If it is specialized, like a poetry anthology, try to select poems that offer a variety of topics and forms.

3. The format can be either of those just described—a simple compilation of the students' handwritten work, or one turned out on a typewriter or computer.

4. A project that represents the work of a semester or entire school year deserves some promotion or publicity. Here are some suggestions for accomplishing this:

   Send a letter home to the parents telling them about the project so they will be alerted to ask their children for the pamphlets when they are distributed.

   Send a short article to your school newspaper, if one exists, describing the project and, perhaps, offering some examples of the students' work.

   Send a press release to your local newspaper, describing the project and attaching a copy of the pamphlet. They may print some of the students' efforts, and may even choose to send a reporter and photographer to your class to do a feature story.

5. Worksheet 9-1A CLASS ANTHOLOGY offers a checklist that will be helpful to the editor(s) of a class anthology.

INDIVIDUAL STUDENT BOOKS

This is a project that students will enjoy. Most young writers love to produce their own books. In some ways, this is even less work for the teacher, since there is no compiling or typing required.

1. Each student will select a writing activity they wish to transform into a book. It can be a story, a collection of poems, or even a nonfiction project.

2. When the piece of writing is ready to be turned into a book, each student, with help from you, if needed, should decide on the format, including size and kind of paper, arrangement of copy, and illustrations. The student has the option to hand-print, write in script, or (if available) utilize a typewriter or computer. Covers can be created of paper or construction paper, and decorated with crayons, felt-tip pens, etc. An effective alternative is to cover cardboard with fabric, wallpaper, foil, or gift wrap. A title and the name of the author should appear on the cover.

3. Worksheet 9-1B WRITE YOUR OWN BOOK offers suggestions to student book authors, including a helpful checklist.

4. Your classroom authors will want others to have the opportunity to see and read their books. You might wish to exhibit the books when they are completed and give all the students time to examine what their classmates have written. Other classes can also be invited to enjoy the books exhibited. This would be an excellent project for part of a parent visiting day.

5. Some teachers have combined this book-writing project with a classroom visit by a published author. After writing their own books, students often discover that an author's comments have a lot more relevance.

Activity 2   WHOLE-SCHOOL PUBLICATIONS

Whole-school publications involve more people, cooperation, intricate planning, and (sometimes) finances than individual class publications. They do, however, offer several advantages. The literary quality can be better since only selected material is included, thus providing a challenge to the more talented or more ambitious students. Also, publication of one's work in a selective vehicle can more effectively validate one's efforts and make the writer feel like a "real" author. Sometimes (in a small school) it is even possible to do a whole-school publication that publishes everyone's work.

If your school already has a newspaper that will consider nonstaff submissions, you can encourage your students to send in material that might be suitable for features, reviews, etc. Some school newspapers even include fiction and poetry. Many schools produce a literary magazine once or twice a year, or even more often. Talented students in your classes can be encouraged to try out for staff positions on these publications. If there are no such publications in your school, the suggestions below may help you initiate one.

SCHOOL NEWSPAPER

1. Discuss with your principal and other interested staff members the feasibility of producing a school newspaper. If the reaction is positive, one of the first decisions that will have to be made is where this activity will fit into the school day and curriculum. Can time be allotted for it during the school day? Would it be preferable to conduct this as an after-school activity? Can it be included in the curriculum as a class in journalism? At least one staff member will have to serve as newspaper advisor or as journalism instructor/advisor.

2. Decisions must also be made regarding name of publication, staff makeup, editorial and submission policies, format, frequency of publication, advertising (if any), budget, and so on. See Chapter 6, "Journalism," for more detailed suggestions on setting up a school newspaper.

3. When the newspaper is in operation, encourage your writing students to submit their best efforts for possible publication. Advise them whether handwritten manuscripts are acceptable or if they must be typed. You can also contact the editor or advisor to ascertain if they are looking for any special topics or types of writing for specific issues, and pass this information along to your writing students.

LITERARY MAGAZINE

1. This is a more specialized type of publication, concentrating primarily on literary forms, and typically including poetry, fiction, memoirs, art work, etc. In many schools, it is produced only once a year, sometimes twice, rarely more often.

2. The standards of literary quality are sometimes higher (or, at least, different) than for a newspaper. This is a place, therefore, for your better writers to submit their work. Those

accepted will have the satisfaction of knowing that their writing is among the best in the school.

3. If there is no literary magazine in your school, you might consider starting one. In general, you can follow the same procedures as suggested for starting a school newspaper. A literary magazine usually requires less effort since it is produced less frequently.

4. Worksheet 9-2 LITERARY MAGAZINE CHECKLIST is helpful for student editors of a new literary magazine.

OTHER WHOLE-SCHOOL WRITING ACTIVITIES

1. An in-school writers' conference for student writers can be an effective tool to encourage creative writing. This conference can take several forms. It can be an all-day effort, or utilize one or more periods. It can be combined with a display of student writing. Teachers can lead workshops in various writing forms, i.e., poetry, journalism, fiction, nonfiction, science fiction. Students can attend all these workshops alternately, or they can be allowed to choose those in which they are most interested. Sometimes, professional authors from the community can be brought in to lead some of these workshops. An excellent follow-up to this activity is to produce a publication including all the work that has been completed as a result of the conference.

2. An "Authors Day" also encourages writing since the "authors" referred to are the students themselves. Usually, this project involves a display of student writing for the entire school body to view, and an all-school or one-grade assembly at which students read some of their work or produce student-written plays. Parents or the community can be invited to attend. This can be an effective time to bring in a guest author to address the students.

Activity 3   DISTRICT-WIDE PUBLICATION ─────────────

Some school districts offer district-wide activities to encourage writing. These can offer even more challenge and greater satisfaction to the ambitious student writer.

1. Some school districts produce a comprehensive publication of student work, usually once a year. If this is available in your district, find out the submission requirements and encourage your students to enter their work where appropriate.

2. Some school systems conduct district-wide contests in various academic and athletic areas. A writing competition is sometimes included, often as part of a special occasion such as a significant town anniversary, holiday, season, etc. Encourage your students to submit their work, or send it in for them.

3. A district-wide writers' conference can be exciting as well as effective in emphasizing the importance of writing. Such a conference would follow the same format as indicated for an in-school writers conference, except that instead of including the entire student body, only those interested in writing would be able to attend. This type of activity is often delegated to the coordinator for gifted and talented instruction, but all young authors who truly desire to attend should be given the opportunity to do so.

Activity 4   SEEKING A WIDER AUDIENCE ─────────────

Serious writing students can aspire to a wider audience than that provided in their school or school district. Here are some suggestions.

COMMUNITY PUBLICATIONS

Sometimes local publications, such as the following, will accept submissions from community members:

1. Newspapers: Your local newspaper often prints letters to the editor, and may be very interested in the point of view of students. Many consider short opinion pieces for the op-ed page. Some newspapers use student correspondents to report on school athletics and other events.

2. Other publications: A local or regional magazine may accept student submissions. Your community may produce a publication to which your students can submit their work.

LOCAL CONTESTS

1. Your local newspaper may occasionally sponsor writing competitions for young people, or report on those sponsored by other groups.

2. Sometimes, community service organizations such as the Junior Chamber of Commerce, Lions Club, Elks, and others may sponsor student writing contests. These are usually geared to specific holidays, events, or patriotic themes. You can enter your students' work, or encourage them to submit entries themselves.

NATIONAL PUBLICATIONS AND CONTESTS

The wider the audience, the more difficult it becomes to get published. Students who wish to do so should be encouraged to submit their best work to national publications. They should be warned to keep in mind, however, that such publications receive many, many submissions, sometimes numbering in the thousands, and cannot possibly publish everything they receive. A rejection from such a publication, therefore, does not mean that the writing is not good, and should be accepted with such an understanding.

There is much fluctuation and change among the publications and contests that accept student work. Those listed below were operating at the time of this writing.

PUBLICATIONS THAT ACCEPT STUDENT WORK

Alive for Young Teens (Christian Board of Publication, Box 179, St. Louis, MO 63166). Fiction, nonfiction, poetry, puzzles, riddles, and tongue-twisters by twelve- to fifteen-year-olds.

Animal Lovers Magazine (Box 918, New Providence, NJ 07974). Animal-related articles, including stories, human interest, humor, personal experience.

Boy's Life Magazine (1325 Walnut Hill Lane, Irving TX 75062). Readers page for interesting ideas, including hobby projects.

Children's Playmate (Youth Publications, P.O. 567B, Indianapolis, IN 46206). For children ages 5–8. Humor and poems.

Clubhouse (Box 15, Berrien Springs, MS 49103). Pays about $10 a poem for children's poetry.

Cricket (P.O. Box 100, LaSalle, IL 61301). For children ages 6–12. Fiction, humor, puzzles, songs, crafts, recipes, light verse, nonsense rhymes.

Crusader Magazine (Box 7244, Grand Rapids, MI 49510). For boys ages 9–14. Material relevant to wholesome interests of boys. Has a Christian perspective.

Current Consumer (Curriculum Innovations, Inc., 501 Lake Forest Ave., Highwood, IL 60040). For junior and senior high students. Articles pertaining to student as consumer. Also accepts puzzles and short humor.

Ebony Jr. (Johnson Publishing Co., 820 S. Michigan Ave., Chicago, IL 60605). Geared toward black children ages 6–12. Nonfiction, fiction, book and movie reviews, poetry, puzzles, games, humor.

Encore (1121 Major Ave. NW, Albuquerque, NM 87107). Poetry.

Fun (P.O. Box 40283, Chicago, IL 60605). For children ages 6–12. Poetry, riddles, letters, stories, and jokes.

Highlights For Children (803 Church St., Honesdale, PA 18431). For children ages 2–12. Nonfiction, science, sports, arts and crafts.

It's Our World (800 Allegheny Ave., Pittsburgh, PA 15233). For children in Catholic elementary schools, ages 6–13. Nonfiction, fiction, poetry.

Jack and Jill (1100 Waterway Blvd., Box 567B, Indianapolis, IN 46206). Stories, poems, riddles, and jokes.

Just About Me (Ensio Industries, 247 Marlee Ave., Suite 206, Toronto, Ontario, Canada M6B 4B8). A magazine for girls ages 12–19. Fiction and poetry.

Kids (Box 2345, Evergreen CO 80439). Fiction, poetry.

Merlyn's Pen, A National Magazine of Student Writing (P.O. Box 1058, East Greenwich, RI 02818). For students grades 7–10. Stories, poems, plays, reviews, letters.

Purple Cow: Atlanta's Magazine for Kids (110 E. Andrews Drive NW, Atlanta, GA 30305). Ages 12–18. Fiction, fillers.

Ranger Rick's Nature Magazine (National Wildlife Federation, 1412 Sixteenth St. NW, Washington, DC 20036). For ages 4–12. Nonfiction, fiction, puzzles.

Reflections (P.O. Box 368, Duncan Falls, OH 43734). Poetry.

Sprint Magazine (Scholastic Magazines, 50 W. 44th Street, New York, NY 10036). For pre-teeners. Fiction, nonfiction, plays, humor.

Stone Soup (P. O. Box 83, Santa Cruz, CA 95063). For children to age 14. Fiction, poetry, art.

Wombat, A Journal of Young People's Writing and Art (365 Ashton Drive, Athens, GA 30606). For ages 6–17. Fiction, poetry, puzzles, humor.

Workman Publishing Company (1 West 39th St., New York, NY 10018). Has published several books by children. For information, write stating ideas, and send a self-addressed envelope for their guidelines.

Young Ambassador (Good News Broadcasting Assn., Inc., Box 82808, Lincoln, NE 68501). For ages 12–16. Short fillers.

Young World (The Saturday Evening Post Co, Youth Division, P.O. Box 567B, Indianapolis, IN 46206). For ages 10–14. Fiction, nonfiction, poetry, puzzles, humor.

CONTESTS OPEN TO STUDENT WRITERS

Contest details often change from year to year. It is suggested, therefore, that you first write to the addresses below requesting rules and applications before submitting work.

Shoe Tree Competition for Young Writers, (National Association for Young Writers, P.O. Box 452, Belvidere, NJ 07823). Fiction, poetry, and nonfiction in two age groups, ages 6–10 and 11–15, cash prizes.

The Cricket Magazine for Children (Cricket League, Box 100, LaSalle, IL 61301). Story contests, age 13 and under.

Make Mine a Mystery Contest (*The Young Writer*, 26409 Timberlane Drive SE, Kent, WA 98042). Mysteries. Three age groups: age 7 and under, 8–11, 12–14. Cash prizes and books.

Name_____ Date_____

CLASS ANTHOLOGY

FOR ANTHOLOGY EDITORS: The following checklist will help you produce your class anthology. Place a check mark in the blank after you complete each step.

Check here
when done

_____ 1. Decide on a title for your anthology. Write it here: _____

_____ 2. Does your anthology have a theme, or will it feature a particular kind of writing, such as fiction, poetry, essays? Write this below. (If there is no theme, write "general.")

_____ 3. Will it be (check one):
　　　____ handwritten　　　　　　　　　　(If typed or word pro-
　　　____ typed　　　　　　　　　　　　　cessed, who will do it?
　　　____ word processed　　　　　　　　　_____)

_____ 4. Write the editors' names below. Next to each name, list that person's responsibilities.

　　　　_____

　　　　_____

　　　　_____

　　　　_____

　　　　_____

_____ 5. What requirements will you have for material to be included? Some of these might be "at least one piece from each student," "equal number of poems and stories," "length limit—two handwritten pages." List your requirements below:

　　　　_____

　　　　_____

　　　　_____

　　　　_____

_____ 5A. Check here when you have completed the selection of material.

_____ 6. Check here when the final pages have been written, typed, or word processed.

_____ 7. Prepare a "Contents" page, containing the name of each selection, author, and pages on which it appears. This can be done alphabetically by title or by author, listed by subject (poems, stories, etc.), or arranged in page order from beginning to end.

(Continued On Next Page)

_____ 8. Prepare a title page. This should include the anthology title, school name, class, teacher, date, and names of editors. Here is a sample:

```
PUMPKIN POEMS
Class 6C        October, 19—
Valley Middle School
Editors: C. James
         P. Guzman
         R. Morrisey
```

_____ 9. Prepare a cover page. This can be made of paper, construction paper, posterboard, or even cardboard covered with fabric, foil, wallpaper, or gift wrap. The anthology name should appear on the cover. You might also wish to include school, class, teacher, and date. Here is one possible cover design.

```
PUMPKIN
  POEMS

Class 6C        October, 19—
Mr. Wolfe        Valley Middle Sch.
```

_____ 10. Do you want to publicize your anthology? Here are some suggestions:

• Send a letter home to students' parents. (They may want extra copies for friends and relatives.)

• Send a letter to a local newspaper describing your project. They may write an article about it or even send a reporter to your class.

• Send copies to other classrooms.

• Post a copy on the bulletin board in the school office.

What will your group do?

_____

_____

_____

_____

_____

Name_____ Date_____

WRITE YOUR OWN BOOK

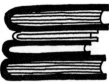

The following list of suggestions will help you write, design, and produce your own book. Place a check mark in the blank after you complete each step.

Check here
when done

_____ 1. Select a writing activity you would like to turn into a book. It can be a story, a poem, a biography, a "how-to" book, a study of dinosaurs, or any other writing project that appeals to you. On the first line below, write the kind of writing activity you have chosen. On the second line, write a title for your book.

(kind of book)_____

(title)_____

_____ 2. Check here when you have completed the final draft (not in book form, just on regular paper).

_____ 3. Decide on the style and form of your book by filling in the blanks below:
Page size _____ Kind of paper _____ (Check one) handwritten _____ typed _____ word processed _____ number of pages _____ Illustrations? _____ On how many pages? _____ Cover (check one): paper _____ construction paper _____ posterboard _____ cardboard covered with fabric _____ cardboard covered with wallpaper _____ cardboard covered with foil _____ cardboard covered with gift wrap _____

_____ 4. Check here when the printing and illustrations are completed and the pages are ready to be put together.

_____ 5. Prepare a title page containing title and name of author. You can also include school, class, date, teacher. Here is a sample title page.

> FLYING SAUCERS
> by
> Kris Wombly
>
> Holland M.S., 6C
> June 19__

_____ 6. Prepare your cover. Include title and author's name as well as any illustrations you wish.

_____ 7. Prepare a back cover. This can be either plain or illustrated. It might be fun to write a "blurb"—a paragraph about the author or the book.

_____ 8. Bind your book together in whatever manner you and your teacher have decided on.

Name_____ Date_____

LITERARY MAGAZINE CHECKLIST

The following checklist will be helpful in producing a literary magazine, especially if you are new at it. Place a checkmark in the blank after you complete each step.

**Check here
when done**

_____ 1. Proposed name of magazine_____

_____ 2. List editors' names below. Next to each name, list each editor's responsibilities (such as art, fiction, poetry, production, advertising, etc.).

_____

_____

_____

_____

_____

_____ 3. Publication date (or dates)_____

_____ 4. How will it be produced? (check one)
handwritten ____ word processed ____ typed ____ printed ____ (If printed, where?) ____

_____ 5. Check kinds of writing that will be included: fiction ____ nonfiction ____ poetry ____ art ____ humor ____

_____ 6. How will you notify students that you are accepting submissions? (Check when done.)
notice on office bulletin board_____
written notice to all teachers_____
written notice to all students_____
announcement on school intercom_____

_____ 7. Write below your guides for selection of work to be included, such as "some work from each grade," "equal amount of poetry and prose," "length limit three handwritten pages," etc.

_____

_____

_____

_____

_____ 8. Deadline for submissions_____

_____ 9. Check here when all selections have been made.

_____ 10. Check here when material has been arranged in final page format.

_____ 11. Prepare a title page, including name of magazine, school, date. (Sample below)

> ## THE LAMPLIGHTER
> Hillside Junior High
> June, 19___

_____ 12. Prepare a staff page listing editors and other staff members. (Sample below)

> Co-Editors: J. Franke
>   R. Shea
> Fiction Editor: L. Meyer
> Poetry Editor: A. Ikeda
> Articles Editor: C. Post
> Art Editor: B. Esposito
> Advertising Editor: L. Garcia
> Production Editor: P. Lee

_____ 13. Prepare a Contents Page, listing each item, author's name, and page on which it appears. This can be arranged alphabetically by title, alphabetically by author, listed by subjects (poetry, fiction, etc.), or in page order from front to back. (Sample below).

> ## IN THIS ISSUE
>
> | | |
> |---|---|
> | The Time Traveler | p. 4 |
> | Sara's Secret | 6 |
> | Butterflies | 7 |
> | Love Song | 7 |
> | The Haunted House | 8 |
> | The Last Inning | 10 |
> | Growing Up | 12 |
> | Weird Dreams | 12 |
> | Hillside Mystery | 13 |
> | Favorite Summer Recipes | 16 |